FEAR ON FIRE

A MIND GAME

By
DEEPAK SHAHI

DEDICATION

To

To my Mum, Mishri Shahi, and Dad, Suresh Karan Shahi - your courage and efforts in navigating a challenging journey from Nepal to India Mumbai have shaped who we are today. With deep gratitude and utmost respect, this book is dedicated to both of you.

TABLE OF CONTENTS

CHAPTER 1

A WORLD GRIPPED BY FEAR

In a world much like our own, fear had become an ever-present companion. This emotion had settled deep within the hearts of every individual, regardless of age, gender, or social standing. It was as if an invisible veil of dread and anxiety had descended upon the planet, casting its long shadow over all aspects of life.

The morning sun filtered through the curtains of an ordinary suburban home, revealing a family of four seated at the breakfast table. Their eyes were glued to the television screen as the news broadcast relayed the day's headlines. Each story seemed to stoke the flames of fear even further, spreading panic and despair like wildfire. Reports of terrorist attacks, natural disasters, and economic crises painted a bleak picture of the world, and the family couldn't help but feel overwhelmed by the sheer weight of it all.

As the father sipped his coffee, he couldn't shake the nagging worry that had taken root: Would he be able to provide for his family in these uncertain times? The mother, in turn, feared for her children's safety and wondered if they could thrive in such a hostile environment. The teenage daughter, already grappling with the challenges of adolescence, felt the added burden of social anxieties and the pressure to succeed academically. The young son, barely old enough to comprehend the complexities of the world, sensed the tension in the air and clung to his mother's side, his tiny heart racing with each passing moment.

Across the globe, similar scenes unfolded in homes, offices, schools, and public spaces. People were haunted by the relentless barrage of bad news and the seemingly insurmountable problems facing humanity. Fear has permeated every aspect of society, influencing the decisions and actions of individuals, communities, and entire nations. It was as if the world was caught in a vicious cycle, with each new crisis amplifying the collective sense of dread.

But amidst the darkness, a flicker of hope began to emerge. A growing number of individuals were starting to question the power that fears held over their lives. As their fears ignited, these brave souls sought to confront and overcome the paralysing force that had held them captive for so long. Unbeknownst to them, their courageous actions would soon set in motion a chain of events that would change the course of history.

In the chapters that follow, we'll explore the lives of various individuals as they navigate this world gripped by fear. From everyday people to influential figures, we'll witness the transformative power of facing one's fears and the impact they can have on the world around us. In a world where fear is on fire, the actions of these courageous individuals will serve as beacons of hope, illuminating the path to a brighter future.

CHAPTER 2

THE TEACHER'S STRUGGLE

Sarah Thompson, a passionate and dedicated middle school teacher, had always believed in the power of education to shape young minds and create a brighter future. However, the world of fear had seeped into the classroom, casting its shadow over her students and fellow teachers alike.

As Sarah prepared for another day of classes, she couldn't help but worry about the mounting pressures her students faced. The high-stakes standardised tests, increasingly competitive college admissions, and the omnipresent threat of bullying and violence had created an environment of constant anxiety. She knew that many of her students were struggling, both academically and emotionally, and she longed to find a way to ease their burdens.

In the teachers' lounge, Sarah's colleagues echoed her concerns. Conversations frequently revolved around job security, budget cuts, and the fear of being held accountable for their student's performance, despite the myriad factors beyond their control. The stress was palpable, and the once-close-knit community of educators felt fragmented and isolated.

Determined to make a difference, Sarah decided to confront her own fears and take action. She recognized that her students needed more than just academic guidance; they needed emotional support and a safe space to express themselves. To that end, she began to incorporate mindfulness and stress management techniques into her lesson plans, teaching her students valuable coping skills to help them navigate the turbulent world around them.

Word of Sarah's innovative approach quickly spread throughout the school, and before long, other teachers were following her lead. As the teachers collaborated and shared their experiences, they began to forge stronger bonds, rekindling the sense of camaraderie and support that had once defined their community.

Inspired by the positive changes in her classroom, Sarah also sought to address the issue of fear on a larger scale. She organised a series of workshops and seminars for parents and educators, focusing on the impact of fear on children's mental health and well-being. These events attracted participants from across the region, sparking a much-needed conversation about the role of fear in education and society at large.

Through her unwavering commitment to her students and her determination to overcome her own fears, Sarah ignited a spark of hope within her community. Little did she know that her actions would soon inspire others to confront their fears and ignite their own flames of change.

CHAPTER 3

A MOTHER'S CONCERN

Across town, in a modest apartment, Maria Alvarez was a single mother doing her best to raise her two young children, Luis and Isabella. Fear had nestled into her heart like an unwelcome guest, keeping her awake at night with worries about her children's safety, their future, and her ability to provide for their needs.

Maria worked long hours at a nearby factory, leaving her children in the care of her elderly mother during the day. The news of escalating crime rates, economic uncertainty, and political instability had made her increasingly fearful for her family's well-being. She found herself obsessing over every little detail, from the food they ate to the routes they took to school, in an attempt to shield her children from the dangers that seemed to lurk around every corner.

One evening, after putting her children to bed, Maria stumbled upon a local news segment featuring Sarah Thompson's workshops on fear and children's mental health. Intrigued by the idea, Maria decided to attend one of the sessions in the hope of finding some solace and guidance.

The workshop proved to be a turning point for Maria. As she listened to Sarah speak about the impact of fear on children and families, she realised that she was not alone in her worries and concerns. The sense of connection she felt with the other parents and educators in the room was a balm to her weary soul, offering a glimmer of hope amidst the darkness.

Empowered by the knowledge and strategies she gained from the workshop, Maria began to confront her own fears head-on. She started by making small, deliberate changes in her daily routine, like taking a different route to work or trying new activities with her children. These small acts of courage helped her break free from the cycle of fear and anxiety that had held her captive.

As Maria grew more confident in her ability to face her fears, she became increasingly involved in her community. She joined a neighbourhood watch group, volunteered at her children's school, and even began organising events to bring her community together. Through her efforts, she ignited a sense of unity and camaraderie among her neighbours, inspiring them to face their own fears and work together for the betterment of their community.

Maria's journey, like that of Sarah Thompson, was just one example of the power of fear on fire. Her courage and determination to create a brighter future for her children and her community served as a beacon of hope, demonstrating that even in a world gripped by fear, the human spirit could still prevail.

CHAPTER 4

THE BUSINESSMAN'S AWAKENING

On the other side of the city, in a gleaming high-rise office building, Adam Johnson sat in his corner office, staring out at the sprawling metropolis below. A successful entrepreneur, he had built his empire from the ground up, driven by ambition and a relentless pursuit of wealth. Yet, as he looked out over the city, he couldn't shake the growing sense of unease that had taken hold of him in recent years.

Adam's fears were rooted in the rapid changes that were transforming the business world. The rise of automation, the unpredictability of the global economy, and the increasing demand for corporate social responsibility weighed heavily on his mind. He worried about the future of his company and the well-being of his employees, many of whom had become like family to him over the years.

One day, during a rare moment of introspection, Adam realised that he had been allowing fear to dictate his actions and decisions for far too long. He recognized that his relentless pursuit of wealth had blinded him to the more significant issues facing the world and had distanced him from his own humanity.

Determined to make a change, Adam began to confront his fears and reassess his priorities. He took a more active role in his employees' well-being, implementing policies that promoted work-life balance and providing resources for their mental and physical health. He also sought to make his company more environmentally sustainable, investing in green technologies and reducing the organisation's carbon footprint.

But Adam's transformation didn't stop there. Inspired by the stories of Sarah Thompson and Maria Alvarez, which he had come across in the local news, he decided to use his wealth and influence to tackle larger social issues. He began collaborating with other business leaders to create a network of socially responsible companies, pooling their resources and expertise to address pressing challenges such as poverty, climate change, and access to education.

As word of Adam's efforts spread, more and more business owners joined the movement, inspired by the idea of using their success for the greater good. Together, they ignited a wave of change that began to reshape the business world, challenging the notion that profit and social responsibility were mutually exclusive.

Through his journey of self-discovery and his commitment to creating a better future, Adam unleashed the power of fear on fire. His transformation served as a testament to the extraordinary potential that lay within every individual, regardless of their circumstances, to make a lasting impact on the world around them.

CHAPTER 5

THE SCIENTIST'S DILEMMA

In a state-of-the-art research facility on the city's outskirts, Dr Emma Larson found herself at a crossroads. As a leading expert in the field of artificial intelligence, she was on the verge of a ground-breaking discovery that could revolutionise the way humans interacted with technology. However, she was also acutely aware of the potential dangers and ethical implications of her work.

Fear bites at Emma's conscience as she contemplates the possible consequences of her research. In the wrong hands, her AI technology could be weaponized or used to manipulate public opinion and undermine democracy. Moreover, the rapid advancement of AI had the potential to disrupt entire industries and displace millions of workers, exacerbating economic inequality and social unrest.

Torn between her passion for scientific discovery and her concerns for the greater good, Emma found herself at an impasse. That was until she stumbled upon an article about the inspiring journeys of Sarah Thompson, Maria Alvarez, and Adam Johnson. Reading about their courageous efforts to confront their fears and create positive change in their communities, Emma felt a renewed sense of purpose and clarity.

Inspired by their examples, Emma decided to confront her own fears and take responsibility for the potential impact of her research. She reached out to colleagues in her field, organising a series of conferences and workshops to discuss the ethical implications of AI and develop guidelines for its responsible development and use. Emma also worked closely with policymakers and business leaders, advocating for regulations that would ensure the safe and equitable integration of AI into society.

In addition to her efforts within the scientific community, Emma sought to educate the public about the benefits and risks of AI. She gave lectures, wrote articles, and participated in panel discussions, demystifying the technology and encouraging a balanced and informed dialogue about its potential applications.

By facing her fears and embracing her responsibility as a scientist, Emma ignited her own fear on fire. Her actions not only helped to shape the future of AI but also inspired others in the scientific community to consider the broader implications of their work. As a result, a new era of responsible and ethical scientific progress began to unfold, driven by individuals who recognized their power to shape the world for the better.

CHAPTER 6

THE JOURNALIST'S QUEST FOR TRUTH

Amidst the bustling newsroom of a prominent city newspaper, Maya Patel worked tirelessly to bring the truth to light. As an investigative journalist, she had witnessed first-hand the power of fear in shaping the stories that dominated the headlines. Sensationalism and fear-mongering had become the norm in journalism, fuelled by a relentless 24-hour news cycle and the unyielding competition for attention.

Maya was growing increasingly disillusioned with the state of her profession. She believed that journalism should serve as a force for good, providing accurate and balanced information to help people make informed decisions. Yet, the constant barrage of alarming headlines and exaggerated stories only seemed to feed the public's anxieties, perpetuating the cycle of fear that gripped the world.

One evening, as Maya sifted through the day's news, she came across the inspiring stories of Sarah Thompson, Maria Alvarez, Adam Johnson, and Dr Emma Larson. Their journeys of confronting their fears and igniting positive change resonated deeply with her. Maya realised that she too had the power to break free from the constraints of fear and use her voice to make a difference.

With renewed determination, Maya decided to challenge the status quo and become a catalyst for change within her industry. She sought out stories that showcased the resilience and strength of the human spirit, highlighting individuals and communities that were overcoming their fears and making a positive impact on the world. Maya also tackled complex and controversial issues, striving to present a balanced and nuanced perspective that empowered readers to form their own opinions.

To amplify her efforts, Maya reached out to other like-minded journalists and media professionals, forming a network dedicated to promoting responsible and ethical journalism. This group of passionate individuals worked together to create guidelines and resources for their peers, fostering a shift towards a more truthful and constructive approach to reporting the news.

As word of Maya's mission spread, more and more journalists began to join the movement, inspired by the opportunity to be part of something greater than themselves. The collective efforts of these fearless reporters helped to reshape the media landscape, slowly replacing fear and sensationalism with hope, understanding, and empathy.

Maya's journey, like those of the individuals who had inspired her, demonstrated the transformative power of fear on fire. By confronting her own fears and challenging the status quo, she sparked a movement that would forever change the way people saw the world and, in turn, the world itself.

CHAPTER 7

THE RIPPLE EFFECT

As news of the remarkable stories of Sarah Thompson, Maria Alvarez, Adam Johnson, Dr Emma Larson, and Maya Patel spread, a wave of inspiration swept through the city and beyond. People from all walks of life began to recognize the power they held within themselves to confront their fears and create positive change in their communities.

Among those touched by these stories was Alex Chen, a young activist who had long been passionate about social justice and environmental issues. Alex had always felt a sense of urgency in addressing the challenges facing the world, but the pervasive atmosphere of fear had often left him feeling overwhelmed and unsure of where to begin.

Inspired by the stories of those who had ignited their fears on fire, Alex realised that the key to making a difference lay in small, consistent actions that could ripple outwards and create lasting change. With renewed Vigor, Alex dove into grassroots activism, organising events, and collaborating with like-minded individuals to raise awareness about critical issues and empower others to take action.

As Alex's efforts gained momentum, more and more people began to join the movement, transforming their own fears into a powerful force for good. Teachers, students, parents, scientists, business owners, journalists, and countless others found the courage to confront their anxieties and become agents of change in their own unique ways.

The ripple effect of these individual actions culminated in a city-wide event called "Fear on Fire Day," organised by Alex and a team of dedicated volunteers. The event featured workshops, panel discussions, and community projects designed to inspire and empower attendees to confront their fears and use them as a catalyst for positive change. Sarah, Maria, Adam, Emma, and Maya were among the keynote speakers, sharing their journeys and encouraging others to follow in their footsteps.

As the sun set on "Fear on Fire Day," a sense of unity and hope filled the hearts of those who had gathered to celebrate their collective courage. They understood that, although fear was an inescapable part of life, they held the power to transform it into something greater – a driving force for change that could reshape the world for the better.

The legacy of "Fear on Fire" continued to grow, inspiring new generations to confront their fears and work together to create a brighter future. In a world once gripped by fear, the flames of courage, resilience, and hope burned brightly, illuminating the path towards a more just and compassionate society.

CHAPTER 8

THE GLOBAL SPARK

As the stories of Sarah Thompson, Maria Alvarez, Adam Johnson, Dr Emma Larson, Maya Patel, and Alex Chen continued to spread, the impact of their collective courage began to reach far beyond their city. The powerful message of "Fear on Fire" resonated with people around the globe, inspiring a new wave of change-makers who were eager to confront their own fears and make a difference.

In a small village in Africa, a courageous young woman named Amina took it upon herself to challenge traditional gender norms and advocate for girls' education. Facing considerable resistance and backlash, Amina persevered, working tirelessly to secure funding, resources, and support for a new school that would provide equal educational opportunities for all children in her community.

Halfway across the world, in a bustling European city, a group of innovative entrepreneurs banded together to create a sustainable, eco-friendly business model that prioritised environmental stewardship and social responsibility. Their groundbreaking approach to commerce quickly gained traction, inspiring other companies to adopt similar practices and paving the way for a greener, more ethical global economy.

Meanwhile, in a conflict-ridden region of the Middle East, a fearless peacemaker named Hassan dedicated his life to promoting dialogue and understanding between warring factions. Despite the seemingly insurmountable challenges he faced, Hassan remained steadfast in his commitment to fostering peace, building bridges of trust and cooperation that would ultimately help to heal the deep wounds of his war-torn homeland.

As these and countless other stories of courage and hope began to emerge, the spirit of "Fear on Fire" spread like wildfire, igniting a global movement that transcended borders, cultures, and ideologies. People everywhere recognized that they were not alone in their fears and that by facing them head-on and working together, they could overcome even the most daunting of challenges.

The transformative power of "Fear on Fire" served as a testament to the resilience and strength of the human spirit. In a world that had once been paralyzed by fear, the flames of courage, empathy, and hope now burned brightly, illuminating the path to a more just, compassionate, and sustainable future for all. And as the ripples of change continued to spread, it became clear that the greatest force for good lay not in the absence of fear, but in the unwavering determination to rise above it and create a better world, one courageous step at a time.

CHAPTER 9

UNITED IN COURAGE

As the "Fear on Fire" movement continued to gain momentum, people from all corners of the world started to recognize their shared humanity and the power they held when they came together. The once seemingly insurmountable divisions that had separated them – whether political, cultural, or ideological – began to fade as they discovered their collective strength.

In response to this global awakening, a group of influential individuals, including Sarah Thompson, Maria Alvarez, Adam Johnson, Dr Emma Larson, Maya Patel, Alex Chen, Amina, and Hassan, decided to organise an international summit called "United in Courage." The event was designed to bring together representatives from every nation, providing a platform for collaboration and the exchange of ideas on how to address the world's most pressing challenges.

During the summit, delegates participated in workshops and panel discussions, exploring topics such as climate change, poverty, inequality, education, and peacebuilding. The atmosphere was electric, as participants from diverse backgrounds and perspectives shared their insights, experiences, and expertise in pursuit of a common goal – a more just, equitable, and sustainable world.

Throughout the event, the spirit of "Fear on Fire" served as a guiding light, reminding everyone in attendance of the power they held within themselves to confront their fears and create positive change. As the delegates engaged in dialogue and debate, they were inspired by the stories of courage and resilience that had brought them together, fuelling their determination to forge a brighter future for all.

By the conclusion of the "United in Courage" summit, a landmark declaration was drafted, outlining a global action plan to address the most pressing challenges facing humanity. This document, which became known as the "Courage Accord," served as a testament to the power of unity and collaboration, providing a blueprint for nations and individuals alike to work together in the pursuit of a better world.

The impact of the summit and the Courage Accord was felt around the globe, as governments, businesses, organisations, and communities began to implement the principles and strategies outlined in the agreement. As they confronted their fears and worked together to create lasting change, the world witnessed a new era of global cooperation, driven by the indomitable human spirit.

In this world united in courage, the flames of hope and resilience burned brighter than ever before, casting away the shadows of fear and illuminating the path towards a more just, compassionate, and sustainable future for all.

CHAPTER 10

A NEW DAWN

Years had passed since the "United in Courage" summit, and the world had undergone a remarkable transformation. The principles of the Courage Accord had been embraced by nations, organisations, and individuals alike, leading to unprecedented levels of cooperation and progress on a global scale.

Climate change, once an existential threat, was now being tackled head-on through innovative solutions and collaborative efforts. Countries had transitioned to renewable energy sources, and businesses had adopted eco-friendly practices, working in harmony with the environment to ensure a sustainable future.

Inequality and poverty, which had long plagued society, were being addressed through comprehensive policies and initiatives. Education and healthcare had become accessible to all, irrespective of their social or economic status, fostering a new era of opportunity and social mobility.

The spirit of peace and understanding that had been championed by individuals like Hassan now flourished across the globe. Conflicts had given way to diplomacy, and former adversaries were now working side by side to address shared challenges and forge a brighter future for all.

As the world continued to evolve, the impact of the "Fear on Fire" movement remained evident in every corner of the globe. The courage, resilience, and hope that had defined the journeys of Sarah, Maria, Adam, Emma, Maya, Alex, Amina, and countless others had inspired generations to confront their fears and embrace their potential for positive change.

It was a new dawn for humanity, a time of unity and progress forged by the power of "Fear on Fire." While challenges and uncertainties would always remain, the indomitable spirit that had fuelled this extraordinary transformation would continue to burn brightly, guiding the world towards a more just, compassionate, and sustainable future.

And as the sun rose on this new world, the legacy of those who had ignited their fears on fire served as a timeless reminder of the extraordinary power that resided within each and every individual – the power to confront fear, to rise above it, and to create a world that was truly united in courage.

CHAPTER 11

THE FEAR WITHIN

As the "Fear on Fire," movement continued to transform the world, it became clear that fear was not only a barrier to progress on a global scale but also a powerful force in shaping personal relationships. Friendships, romantic relationships, and family dynamics were all susceptible to the detrimental effects of fear, which could manifest in various forms, such as insecurity, jealousy, and mistrust.

Sophia, a young woman in her twenties, was all too familiar with the impact that fear could have on her relationships. Growing up in a world where fear was pervasive, she had developed a deep-seated fear of rejection and abandonment that had shaped her interactions with others. This fear had led her to become overly cautious in forming connections and to hold back from expressing her true feelings, ultimately hindering her ability to develop deep and meaningful relationships.

Realising that her fear was preventing her from experiencing the joy and fulfilment that comes from genuine connection, Sophia decided to take inspiration from the "Fear on Fire" movement and confront her fear head-on. She began attending therapy sessions and working on self-awareness, and self-acceptance. By facing her fear and understanding its root causes, Sophia gradually learned to let go of her insecurities and open herself up to the possibility of love and friendship.

As Sophia embarked on this journey of self-discovery, she found that she was not alone in her struggle. Many others, including her close friends and family members, were also grappling with fears that had taken a toll on their personal relationships. Inspired by Sophia's progress, they too decided to confront their fears, seeking support and guidance from therapy, support groups, and self-help resources.

Over time, the bonds between Sophia and her loved ones began to strengthen as they collectively worked to overcome their fears. Trust, empathy, and understanding replaced insecurity, jealousy, and mistrust, paving the way for deeper and more meaningful connections.

As word of their experiences spread, the impact of fear on personal relationships became a central theme in the "Fear on Fire" movement. People around the world started to recognize the power that fears held over their relationships, and they too began to face their fears and work towards healthier, more fulfilling connections.

By confronting their fears and embracing vulnerability, people everywhere discovered the transformative power of love, trust, and understanding. In a world where fear had once driven people apart, the flames of "Fear on Fire" now brought them closer together, igniting a new era of connection and unity.

CHAPTER 12

BUILDING BRIDGES

As the impact of "Fear on Fire" continued to reshape personal relationships around the world, communities began to explore the potential of this powerful movement to bridge divides and foster understanding among diverse groups. In a society where fear had once fuelled prejudice, discrimination, and division, people now sought to create a more inclusive and harmonious environment.

In a small, multicultural town, a group of residents decided to establish the "Building Bridges" initiative. Inspired by the principles of the "Fear on Fire" movement, the goal of this initiative was to break down barriers and cultivate connections among individuals from different backgrounds, cultures, and beliefs.

The organisers of the "Building Bridges" initiative planned a series of events and activities designed to bring people together and promote understanding. These events included cultural exchange programs, where participants could learn about each other's customs and traditions; open dialogues, where community members could share their perspectives and engage in constructive discussions; and collaborative projects, where people could work together to address common challenges and improve their community.

As the "Building Bridges" initiative gained momentum, the town witnessed a remarkable transformation. Fear and mistrust were replaced by empathy, respect, and a sense of unity, as people from all walks of life joined forces to create a more inclusive and compassionate community.

The success of the "Building Bridges" initiative caught the attention of other communities around the world, inspiring them to launch similar programs in their own towns and cities. By confronting their fears and embracing the principles of the "Fear on Fire" movement, these communities worked together to build a brighter, more inclusive future for all.

As the world continued to evolve, the impact of "Fear on Fire" on personal relationships and community dynamics served as a powerful reminder of the potential for positive change when people come together, united by their courage and determination to rise above fear. In a world once divided by fear and prejudice, the flames of "Fear on Fire" now burned brightly, illuminating the path towards understanding, unity, and love.

CHAPTER 13

A SPARK OF HOPE

The power of the "Fear on Fire" movement had touched every aspect of life, from personal relationships to entire communities. The world had embraced the idea of confronting fears and working together to create a brighter future. Amidst the progress, however, new challenges and fears began to emerge.

In a remote corner of the world, a previously unknown virus had begun to spread rapidly, causing panic and uncertainty among the population. Fearful of the unknown and the potential consequences of the outbreak, people found themselves struggling with a new wave of anxiety and trepidation.

As news of the virus reached the global community, the heroes of the "Fear on Fire" movement knew that they had a crucial role to play in addressing this new challenge. Harnessing the lessons they had learned and the principles that had guided them, they sprang into action, determined to confront this new fear and provide hope and support to those affected.

Dr Emma Larson, with her background in medical research, led a team of scientists working tirelessly to understand the virus and develop potential treatments and vaccines. Meanwhile, Amina, who had championed girls' education in her village, used her influence to spread accurate information about the virus and promote preventive measures, ensuring that communities were well-informed and prepared to protect themselves and their loved ones.

At the same time, Hassan, the peacemaker from the Middle East, worked to bring together international leaders and organisations to pool resources and coordinate a global response to the crisis. He recognized that only through unity and collaboration could the world overcome this new challenge.

As the fight against the virus continued, the "Fear on Fire" movement once again proved to be a beacon of hope and resilience. People around the world came together, united in their determination to confront their fears and support one another during this difficult time. They drew strength from the stories of courage and perseverance that had defined the "Fear on Fire" movement, reminding themselves that they could overcome even the most daunting of challenges.

In the face of this new threat, the world found solace in the knowledge that fear could be conquered, and that hope and unity would ultimately prevail. As the flames of "Fear on Fire" continued to burn brightly, they cast a light on the indomitable human spirit, providing a spark of hope in the darkness and illuminating the path towards a better tomorrow

33

CHAPTER 14

TRIUMPH OVER ADVERSITY

As the world continued its battle against the virus, the collective efforts of the "Fear on Fire" heroes and the global community began to bear fruit. Dr Emma Larson's team, working in collaboration with scientists from around the world, successfully developed a vaccine that proved effective in protecting against the virus. Governments, businesses, and organisations rallied together to ensure the vaccine was distributed quickly and equitably to all who needed it.

Simultaneously, Amina's efforts to educate communities about the virus and its prevention empowered individuals to take necessary precautions, reducing the spread of the virus and minimising its impact. Hassan's coordination of international resources and support ensured that countries most in need received the assistance required to combat the outbreak.

As the world gradually gained control over the virus, it became evident that the principles of the "Fear on Fire" movement had been instrumental in overcoming this new challenge. The courage, resilience, and unity demonstrated by the global community in the face of adversity had proven that fear could indeed be conquered, even in the most trying of circumstances.

With the threat of the virus subsiding, the world began to rebuild and recover. The lessons learned during the crisis served as a powerful reminder of the importance of collaboration, empathy, and shared responsibility in addressing the challenges that face humanity. Communities that had come together to support one another in their time of need continued to work together, forging stronger bonds and creating a more compassionate and inclusive society.

The triumph over adversity showcased the transformative power of the "Fear on Fire" movement, as people from all walks of life joined forces to confront their fears and create a brighter future. As the world moved forward, the indomitable spirit of "Fear on Fire" served as a beacon of hope and a testament to the extraordinary resilience of the human spirit.

In a world where fear had once held sway, the flames of "Fear on Fire" now burned brighter than ever before, illuminating the path towards a more just, compassionate, and united future for all.

CHAPTER 15

SUSTAINING THE FLAME

In the aftermath of the global triumph over the virus, the world emerged stronger and more united than ever. The "Fear on Fire" movement, which had played a pivotal role in fostering courage, resilience, and unity during the crisis, continued to inspire people across the globe to confront their fears and work towards a better future.

Recognizing the importance of sustaining the momentum of the movement, the "Fear on Fire" heroes and their allies turned their attention to ensuring that the principles and lessons of "Fear on Fire" would be passed down to future generations. They understood that while the world had made significant progress, there would always be new challenges and fears to confront.

To preserve the legacy of the movement, the "Fear on Fire" heroes established the Fear on Fire Foundation. The Foundation aimed to promote the principles of courage, resilience, and unity through education, advocacy, and community engagement. They developed resources and programs to teach children and young adults about the importance of confronting their fears and working together to create a brighter future.

The Foundation also organised events and initiatives to celebrate the power of "Fear on Fire" and showcase inspiring stories of individuals who had confronted their fears and transformed their lives. These events served as a reminder of the potential that resides within each person to rise above fear and make a difference in the world.

As the years went by, the Fear on Fire Foundation became an influential force for change, empowering people across the globe to embrace their fears and unite in the pursuit of a more just, compassionate, and sustainable world. The lessons of "Fear on Fire" continued to resonate with each new generation, fuelling an enduring flame of courage, resilience, and unity that guided humanity through the challenges and uncertainties of the future.

In a world that had once been held captive by fear, the flames of "Fear on Fire" now burned eternally, illuminating the path towards a brighter future and serving as a testament to the extraordinary power of the human spirit to triumph over adversity and forge a world united in

CHAPTER 16

THE POWER STRUGGLE

US and China's Fear-Fueled Race for Global Dominance"
In this chapter, we delve deeper into the various sectors
where the US and China are fiercely competing, driven
by the philosophy of "Fear on Fire." This intense rivalry
has manifested in several key areas, including the
economy, technology, military prowess, and even
cultural influence.

Economy:

Both nations have been racing to achieve the largest
GDP and secure the title of the world's leading economy.
The US, long seen as the global economic powerhouse,
now faces increasing competition from China's rapidly
growing economy. The ongoing trade wars and tariff
battles between the two countries exemplify their
economic struggle for dominance.

Technology:

The US and China are constantly vying for
technological supremacy, particularly in fields like
artificial intelligence, telecommunications, and space
exploration. The competition to develop cutting-edge
technologies and establish global standards has become

increasingly crucial in determining which country will hold the mantle of technological leader.

Military Prowess:

As the US and China compete for global influence, both nations have been investing heavily in their military capabilities. The race to develop advanced weapons systems, expand their naval presence, and establish military bases worldwide demonstrates the critical role that military power plays in their ongoing struggle for dominance.

Cultural Influence:

In addition to economic, technological, and military competition, the US and China are also vying for cultural influence on the global stage. Both countries have been promoting their respective cultures and values through various means, including media, education, and diplomacy.

Throughout this chapter, we explore the complex dynamics of this high-stakes rivalry, presenting interesting facts and analysis of how the "Fear on Fire" philosophy has fueled the competition between these two global giants. We also discuss the potential consequences of this power struggle, as the international community must navigate the delicate balance of power in an increasingly interconnected and rapidly changing world.

CHAPTER 17

THE GLOBAL IMPACT

As the years passed, the "Fear on Fire" movement and the Fear on Fire Foundation continued to grow and evolve, leaving a lasting impact on communities around the globe. The heroes, who had once set out on their individual journeys to confront their fears, had inspired a revolution that transformed the world.

Across nations, the principles of courage, resilience, and unity took root, creating a more compassionate and connected global society. Governments, organisations, and individuals collaborated to address pressing issues, such as poverty, inequality, and climate change, driven by the conviction that together, they could overcome even the most daunting challenges.

The global impact of the "Fear on Fire" movement was evident in the countless stories of people who had confronted their fears and made a difference in their communities. From the young girl who defied societal expectations to become the first female astronaut in her country, to the entrepreneur who developed innovative solutions to provide clean water to remote villages, the world was filled with living examples of the power of "Fear on Fire."

As the movement continued to spread, it became clear that the "Fear on Fire" phenomenon had transcended borders and cultures, uniting people of all backgrounds in their quest to create a brighter future. The flames of "Fear on Fire" ignited a spark within the human spirit, setting the world ablaze with hope, determination, and an unwavering belief in the power of unity.

The legacy of the "Fear on Fire" heroes and the Foundation lived on through the generations, serving as a reminder that the courage to confront one's fears could inspire a global movement capable of transforming the world. From the humble beginnings of individual journeys, the flames of "Fear on Fire" had grown into a powerful force that illuminated the path towards a more just, compassionate, and unified future for all.

CHAPTER 18

MANDELA AND THE FEAR ON FIRE MOVEMENT

Nelson Mandela's fight against apartheid in South Africa was indeed a powerful example of harnessing the energy of fear to bring about monumental change. As a leader in the struggle for racial equality, Mandela's fearless determination to dismantle the oppressive apartheid system inspired millions and eventually led to South Africa's freedom from British rule. Through his unwavering commitment and the use of nonviolent resistance, Mandela managed to ignite the "Fear on Fire" spirit in his followers, turning fear into a driving force for change and progress. This ultimately paved the way for a new era of democracy and social justice in South Africa, showcasing the transformative power of facing fear head-on and using it as fuel for positive action.

CHAPTER 19

ABRAHAM LINCOLN AND THE FIGHT FOR FREEDOM

Abraham Lincoln, the 16th President of the United States, is often celebrated for his role in the abolition of slavery. During his presidency, he faced immense fear and opposition from many quarters, particularly from those who wanted to maintain the institution of slavery. Lincoln's fear stemmed from the possibility of a divided nation, the potential for widespread violence, and the uncertain future for millions of enslaved people.

Despite these fears, Lincoln's determination to address the issue of slavery led to the Emancipation Proclamation in 1863, which declared that all slaves in Confederate-held territories were to be set free. This marked a significant turning point in the fight against slavery and paved the way for the 13th Amendment to the United States Constitution, which officially abolished slavery in 1865.

Lincoln's actions can be seen as an example of the "Fear on Fire" movement, as he confronted his fears head-on and used them as a catalyst for change. His leadership and the abolition of slavery had a profound impact on the lives of millions of African Americans and set the stage for the civil rights movement that would follow in the 20th century. This historic event serves as a powerful reminder of how confronting fear can lead to monumental progress and social transformation.

They recognized that it was time to pass the torch to the next generation of leaders who would carry the legacy of the movement forward.

The Fear on Fire Foundation took on the responsibility of identifying and nurturing young individuals with the potential to become future heroes. They established mentorship programs, connecting the original heroes with these young trailblazers to share their knowledge, experience, and wisdom.

In this new era, the original heroes found renewed purpose in guiding the next generation. Dr Emma Larson mentored a young scientist, who would one day make groundbreaking discoveries in the field of medicine. Amina shared her experiences with a group of young activists determined to advance gender equality around the world.

Hassan guided a young diplomat, imparting lessons on the importance of empathy, understanding, and collaboration in international relations. Alex inspired a new generation of environmentalists, teaching them the importance of respecting the earth and working together to preserve it for future generations.

As the torch was passed to this new generation of heroes, the original heroes took pride in the lasting impact of the "Fear on Fire" movement. They had faced their fears, ignited a global revolution, and now had the privilege of witnessing the next generation continue their legacy.

Through their mentorship and guidance, the original heroes ensured that the principles of courage, resilience, and unity that had defined the "Fear on Fire" movement would live on in the hearts and minds of the young leaders they had helped to shape. The flame of "Fear on Fire" continued to burn brightly, its light casting a warm glow on the future of humanity, illuminating a path of hope, compassion, and unity for generations to come.

CHAPTER 20

THE EVERLASTING FLAME

As the years turned into decades, the impact of the "Fear on Fire" movement only grew stronger. The original heroes, now revered as pioneers of change, had witnessed the world's transformation, and their legacy lived on through the new generation of heroes they had mentored.

The Fear on Fire Foundation expanded its reach, with local chapters established in communities across the globe. Each chapter carried the torch of the "Fear on Fire" movement, addressing local and regional challenges while promoting the principles of courage, resilience, and unity.

In this era of interconnectedness, people from all corners of the world came together to share their experiences, knowledge, and resources, working collaboratively to build a brighter, more sustainable future. The movement had transcended cultural, social, and political barriers, forging a bond of unity and understanding that stretched across the globe.

New heroes continued to emerge, inspired by the stories of their predecessors and the everlasting flame of the "Fear on Fire" movement. They dared to confront their fears, push the boundaries of human potential, and work tirelessly to create positive change in their communities and the world at large.

The "Fear on Fire" movement had become an indelible part of human history, a testament to the extraordinary power of courage, resilience, and unity in the face of fear. Its flame burned eternally, a beacon of hope, inspiration, and determination that would guide and empower generations to come.

In a world that had once been gripped by fear, the "Fear on Fire" movement now stood as a shining example of what humanity could achieve when it chose to confront its fears and work together to create a better future. As the everlasting flame continued to burn, it illuminated the path forward, inspiring the world to keep moving towards a brighter, more compassionate, and united tomorrow.

CHAPTER 21

THE LABOURER'S LAMENT

In the 21st-century world of work, fear often manifested itself in the lives of labourers. They faced job insecurity, harsh working conditions, and the constant threat of being replaced by automation. Despite these challenges, many labourers held onto their jobs with determination, knowing that their families depended on their income.

The "Fear on Fire" movement recognized the struggles of these workers and sought to address their fears by promoting better working conditions, fair wages, and job security. As the movement gained momentum, labour unions and organisations joined forces to amplify the voices of these workers and advocate for their rights.

Across industries, workers began to stand up for themselves, inspired by the "Fear on Fire" principles of courage, resilience, and unity. They demanded safer work environments, fair pay, and opportunities for growth and advancement. In turn, employers started to recognize the value of a motivated and empowered workforce, and they began to implement changes that improved the lives of their employees.

As the "Fear on Fire" movement spread its message of courage and resilience, labourers from all walks of life found the strength to confront their fears, knowing that they were not alone in their struggles. They began to work together, forming a united front to push for a better, more equitable world of work.

This chapter follows the journey of a labourer named Victor, who, inspired by the "Fear on Fire" movement, confronts his fears and takes a stand for better working conditions in his workplace. Victor's story serves as a testament to the power of courage and resilience in the face of adversity, and his actions inspire others in his community to take similar stands, igniting a wave of change that ripples throughout the workforce.

CHAPTER 22

THE MANAGER'S BALANCING ACT

In the fast-paced and demanding world of business, managers often found themselves juggling various responsibilities and expectations. With the pressure to meet targets, manage teams, and satisfy the demands of upper management, fear could take root in the form of stress, anxiety, and self-doubt.

The "Fear on Fire" movement acknowledged the unique challenges faced by managers and emphasised the importance of confronting fear in the workplace. Encouraged by the movement's message, managers began to adopt strategies that fostered a positive, supportive work environment, balancing the needs of their employees with the demands of the business.

In this chapter, we follow the story of Sarah, a middle manager who struggles with the fear of failure and the pressure to perform at work. As she learns about the "Fear on Fire" movement, Sarah discovers new ways to address her fears and create a more balanced, inclusive work environment for her team.

Sarah introduces open communication channels, encourages team-building activities, and advocates for mental health support in the workplace. By confronting her fears and implementing these changes, Sarah not only improves her own well-being but also contributes to a healthier, more supportive work culture.

As the "Fear on Fire," movement continues to spread, Sarah's story inspires other managers to confront their fears and prioritise the well-being of their teams, leading to a more compassionate and successful workplace for all.

CHAPTER 23

THE ENTREPRENEURS LEAP OF FAITH

Entrepreneurs, with their innovative ideas and risk-taking spirit, played a vital role in shaping the economy and driving progress. However, they also faced immense pressure and uncertainty, as the success of their ventures was never guaranteed. Fear could manifest as self-doubt, financial worries, or concerns about the future.

The "Fear on Fire" movement recognized the unique challenges faced by entrepreneurs and encouraged them to confront their fears, embrace failure as a learning opportunity, and persevere through adversity. Inspired by the movement, entrepreneurs began to approach their ventures with renewed courage, resilience, and determination.

In this, we follow the story of Li, a young entrepreneur who dreams of launching a sustainable fashion brand. Plagued by fear and uncertainty, Li hesitates to take the leap and invest in her vision. However, after learning about the "Fear on Fire" movement, Li finds the courage to confront her fears and take the first steps towards bringing her dream to life.

As Li embarks on her entrepreneurial journey, she faces numerous challenges, including securing funding, building a team, and navigating the competitive landscape of the fashion industry. Guided by the principles of the "Fear on Fire" movement, Li perseveres through these obstacles and gradually builds a successful, sustainable business that reflects her values.

Li's story serves as an inspiration to other aspiring entrepreneurs, demonstrating the power of courage, resilience, and determination in overcoming fear and achieving one's dreams. As the "Fear on Fire" movement continues to spread, more entrepreneurs embrace the opportunity to face their fears and pursue their passions, fostering innovation and positive change across industries.

CHAPTER 24

THE CEO'S BURDEN

At the top of the corporate hierarchy, CEOs grappled with enormous responsibilities, making decisions that impacted the lives of employees, shareholders, and consumers. The weight of these responsibilities could give rise to fear, as CEOs face the constant pressure to perform, adapt, and navigate the complexities of an ever-changing business landscape.

The "Fear on Fire" movement emphasised the importance of confronting fear at all levels of society, including the boardroom. Inspired by the movement, CEOs began to reassess their leadership styles, incorporating the principles of courage, resilience, and unity to create more compassionate and effective organisations.

This chapter follows the story of Priya, a CEO who struggles with the fear of making the wrong decisions and jeopardising the future of her company. After discovering the "Fear on Fire" movement, Priya decides to confront her fears and implement changes that promote a more inclusive, transparent, and responsible corporate culture.

Under Priya's leadership, the company became more open to innovation and collaboration, prioritising the well-being of its employees and the communities it serves. By embracing the principles of the "Fear on Fire" movement, Priya not only improves her company's performance but also sets an example for other CEOs to follow.

Priya's story illustrates the powerful impact that fearless leadership can have on an organisation and the wider business world. As the "Fear on Fire," movement continues to spread, it encourages more leaders like Priya to confront their fears, embrace change, and foster a more compassionate, resilient, and united corporate landscape.

CHAPTER 25

THE FREELANCER'S TREPIDATION

The rise of the gig economy and remote work provided new opportunities for individuals seeking flexibility and independence in their careers. Freelancers, navigating the uncertainty of fluctuating income and the constant search for new clients, often faced their own unique set of fears, from financial instability to feelings of isolation.

The "Fear on Fire" movement acknowledged the challenges faced by freelancers and offered support and encouragement to help them confront their fears and thrive in their chosen paths. Empowered by the movement, freelancers began to develop strategies for managing their fears and cultivating resilience in their professional lives.

This chapter tells the story of Miguel, a talented graphic designer who has chosen the freelance life but is plagued by the fear of financial insecurity and the pressure to constantly find new projects. As he learns about the "Fear on Fire" movement, Miguel finds the courage to confront his fears and embrace his chosen career with confidence.

Miguel takes steps to diversify his income, network with other professionals, and establish a support system to help him navigate the challenges of freelancing. By applying the principles of courage, resilience, and unity to his own life, Miguel not only improves his own circumstances but also inspires other freelancers to face their fears and find success in the gig economy.

As the "Fear on Fire," movement spreads, more freelancers like Miguel are empowered to confront their fears and build sustainable, fulfilling careers. By embracing the core principles of the movement, they contribute to a more resilient, adaptable, and innovative workforce, ready to tackle the challenges of the modern world.

CHAPTER 26

THE SCIENTIST'S CONUNDRUM

In their pursuit of knowledge and progress, scientists often faced ethical dilemmas, resource constraints, and the pressure to produce groundbreaking results. The fear of failure, criticism, or the misuse of their research could weigh heavily on their shoulders, influencing their decisions and the direction of their work.

The "Fear on Fire" movement recognized the unique challenges faced by scientists and encouraged them to confront their fears while maintaining a commitment to ethical, responsible research. Inspired by the movement, scientists began to approach their work with renewed courage and dedication, while fostering an environment of collaboration and open dialogue.

In this chapter, we follow the story of Dr Amina, a brilliant researcher whose groundbreaking work in genetic engineering has the potential to revolutionise medicine. However, she is haunted by the fear of her research being misused or causing unintended harm. As Dr Amina learns about the "Fear on Fire" movement, she finds the strength to confront her fears and address the ethical implications of her work.

Driven by the principles of courage, resilience, and unity, Dr Amina forms a multidisciplinary team to address the ethical concerns and potential societal impacts of her research. By doing so, she not only ensures that her work is conducted responsibly but also encourages a culture of collaboration and open discussion within the scientific community.

Dr Amina's story demonstrates the importance of confronting fear in the pursuit of scientific progress and the potential for positive change when researchers embrace the principles of the "Fear on Fire" movement. As the movement continues to spread, more scientists are inspired to face their fears and work together to advance knowledge responsibly, paving the way for a brighter future.

CHAPTER 27

THE EDUCATORS RESOLVE

Educators held a critical role in shaping the minds of future generations, but they often faced their own set of fears, such as the pressure to meet performance standards, navigate changing curricula, and address the diverse needs of their students. The fear of failing their students or not making a meaningful impact could be a heavy burden to bear.

The "Fear on Fire" movement recognized the challenges faced by educators and encouraged them to confront their fears while striving to create inclusive, supportive learning environments. Inspired by the movement, teachers began to develop innovative teaching methods, prioritise emotional intelligence, and promote open communication within their classrooms.

In this chapter, we follow the story of Mr Chen, a dedicated teacher who is passionate about making a difference in his students' lives but struggles with the fear of not living up to their expectations. As Mr Chen discovers the "Fear on Fire" movement, he finds the courage to confront his fears and adopt new teaching strategies that better serve his students.

Embracing the principles of courage, resilience, and unity, Mr Chen creates a classroom culture that encourages collaboration, critical thinking, and emotional growth. By doing so, he not only enhances his students' educational experiences but also helps them develop the skills they need to confront their own fears and challenges in the future.

Mr Chen's story highlights the powerful impact that fearless educators can have on the lives of their students and the importance of fostering resilience and courage in the classroom. As the "Fear on Fire," movement continues to spread, more educators are inspired to confront their fears and contribute to the cultivation of a more compassionate, resilient, and empowered generation.

CHAPTER 28

THE JAPAN'S DEFENCE SPENDING

In this chapter, we examine the growing concerns in Japan regarding regional security and the impact of the "Fear on Fire" philosophy on its defence spending. After the devastation of Hiroshima and Nagasaki during World War II, Japan had largely focused on its economic growth rather than heavily investing in its military capabilities. The security guarantee provided by the United States allowed Japan to maintain a relatively limited defence budget.

However, as regional tensions have intensified in recent years, Japan has felt increasing pressure to enhance its military capabilities. The rise of China as a global power, along with the unpredictable actions of North Korea, has caused Japan to reassess its defence strategy. The ongoing dispute over Taiwan and China's determination to confront the US and its allies further exacerbates the situation in the region.

As a result of the growing fear and uncertainty, Japan's defence spending has seen a significant increase. Between 2018 and 2023, Japan's defence budget has risen from $40 billion to $52 billion, highlighting the nation's shift in priorities. This escalation in defence spending can be attributed to the "Fear on Fire" phenomenon, as Japan attempts to protect its interests and assert its presence in the face of mounting regional threats.

In this chapter, we explore the various factors contributing to Japan's growing defence budget and the implications of this trend for the nation and the broader Asia-Pacific region. We also discuss the potential consequences of Japan's increased military focus and how the international community may respond to this changing dynamic.

CHAPTER 29

THE ARTIST IN A DIGITAL AGE

In this chapter, we delve into the world of artists and the unique fears they face in their creative endeavours. The power of art to provoke thought and inspire emotion has long been recognized as a vital force in shaping culture and society. However, artists often grapple with their own fears, such as the fear of rejection, criticism, or not being able to express their creative vision.

The advent of advanced technologies, such as artificial intelligence (AI) and digital tools, has further complicated the landscape for artists. While these technologies have enabled new forms of expression and expanded the reach of artistic works, they have also raised concerns about the value and authenticity of art created by or with the help of AI systems. As a result, artists may fear being overshadowed by these new technologies or struggling to maintain their relevance in an increasingly digital world.

In this chapter, we explore the challenges and opportunities that the digital age presents for artists, as well as the ways in which the "Fear on Fire" philosophy can help them navigate these uncertainties. We discuss the impact of AI and digital tools on artistic expression and the evolving nature of the art world. We also examine how artists can harness their fears to drive their creativity and thrive in the face of change, as they continue to shape culture and society through their unique visions.

In this chapter, we follow the story of Amir, a talented painter who struggles with the fear of not being understood or appreciated by his audience. As he learns about the "Fear on Fire" movement, Amir finds the courage to confront his fears and fully embrace his artistic vision, unencumbered by self-doubt.

Guided by the principles of courage, resilience, and unity, Amir creates a series of bold, thought-provoking paintings that challenge societal norms and spark meaningful conversations. By doing so, he not only gains recognition for his work but also inspires other artists to confront their fears and express their authentic selves.

Amir's story highlights the transformative power of confronting fear in the realm of artistic expression and the potential for change when artists embrace the principles of the "Fear on Fire" movement. As the movement continues to spread, more artists are inspired to face their fears, pushing the boundaries of creativity and fostering a more vibrant, diverse cultural landscape.

CHAPTER 30

THE HEALER'S COMPASSION

Healthcare professionals, entrusted with the care of their patients, faced immense responsibility and pressure. They grappled with the fear of making mistakes, failing to save a life, or navigating the complexities of the healthcare system. These fears could impact their ability to provide the best possible care for their patients.

The "Fear on Fire" movement acknowledged the unique challenges faced by healthcare professionals and encouraged them to confront their fears while maintaining a commitment to compassion, empathy, and patient-centred care. Inspired by the movement, doctors, nurses, and other healthcare workers began to cultivate resilience and foster supportive, collaborative environments within their workplaces.

In this chapter, we follow the story of Dr Sofia, a dedicated physician who strives to provide the best care for her patients but is burdened by the fear of failure and the pressure to meet ever-increasing demands. As Dr Sofia learns about the "Fear on Fire" movement, she finds the courage to confront her fears and seek ways to improve her practice and patient outcomes.

Embracing the principles of courage, resilience, and unity, Dr Sofia forms a collaborative team with her colleagues, focusing on patient-centred care and open communication. By doing so, she not only enhances the quality of care for her patients but also contributes to a more compassionate, supportive healthcare system.

Dr Sofia's story demonstrates the power of confronting fear in the pursuit of healing and the potential for positive change when healthcare professionals embrace the principles of the "Fear on Fire" movement. As the movement continues to spread, more healthcare workers are inspired to face their fears and work together to create a more compassionate, resilient, and effective healthcare system.

CHAPTER 31

THE POLITICIAN'S DILEMMA

In the world of politics, leaders faced immense responsibilities and pressures as they made decisions that impacted the lives of their constituents and shaped the direction of their countries. Fear could play a significant role in these decisions, whether it was the fear of losing power, failing to meet expectations, or making choices that could have unintended consequences.

A few years back, Europe was relatively relaxed on matters of defence, trade, and energy. With a bloc of 30 countries in the EU, the think tanks might have anticipated risks from Russia. However, they never realised it could come so soon. After the war in Ukraine, the whole dynamic of world power is about to change. Every country on this planet is now in a race to buy weapons, make alliances, and strategize for a potential third world war.

The fear has made defence the topmost priority for countries, prompting them to form alliances with stronger partners. The "Fear on Fire" momentum has taken an SOS mode. Politicians are on high alert, making decisions at a war footing level. The mindset has become "now or never." Just two years ago, apart from a few countries like China, India, France, the UK, Japan, and South Korea, most countries were reluctant to upgrade their defence systems and budgets.

Every sector is directly or indirectly affected by the Russian invasion of the sovereign nation of Ukraine. The political climate has shifted rapidly, and the fear of escalating conflict has become a tangible reality. Countries previously focused on trade and diplomacy are now investing heavily in military capabilities and forging alliances to ensure their security.

Additionally, politicians face public scrutiny and pressure to make decisions that protect their nations while balancing international relations. The fear of making the wrong choice, alienating allies, or escalating tensions can lead to a cautious approach or even indecision. This fear can result in missed opportunities or delayed action, both of which can have long-lasting consequences.

In conclusion, the "Fear on Fire" phenomenon has significantly impacted political decision-making and international relations. As politicians grapple with the responsibility of protecting their countries and navigating the complexities of an increasingly volatile global landscape, fear continues to play a crucial role in shaping their decisions. It is essential for leaders to recognize and manage these fears to make informed choices that best serve their constituents and maintain peace and stability in an increasingly uncertain world.

The "Fear on Fire" movement recognized the unique challenges faced by politicians and statesmen and encouraged them to confront their fears while staying true to their principles and the needs of their people. Inspired by the movement, political leaders began to reassess their priorities, focus on long-term solutions, and foster a culture of collaboration and transparency in their governments.

In this chapter, we follow the story of Minister Anya, a dedicated public servant who is passionate about making a difference in her country but is plagued by the fear of making the wrong decisions or facing backlash from her constituents. As she learns about the "Fear on Fire" movement, Anya finds the courage to confront her fears and stay true to her vision for a better future.

Minister Anya's story illustrates the power of confronting fear in the realm of politics and the potential for positive change when leaders embrace the principles of the "Fear on Fire" movement. As the movement continues to spread, more politicians are inspired to face their fears, work together, and make decisions that prioritise the well-being of their citizens and the greater good.

CHAPTER 32

A NATION DIVIDED

In a world where fear permeated the lives of individuals from all walks of life, it also played a significant role in shaping the political landscape. Countries faced deep divisions along ideological lines, fueled by fear-mongering tactics that pitted citizens against one another, exacerbating social tensions and obstructing progress.

Mayor Jacob, a charismatic leader of a divided city, faced the challenge of bringing harmony to a community torn apart by competing factions. Each group was driven by their own fears and insecurities, which had brought progress to a standstill. Here, we explore some vivid illustrations of the day-to-day life in the city that capture the attention of its citizens and offer practical examples to implement in their daily lives.

Traffic Gridlock: One of the city's most pressing issues was the constant traffic gridlock. Mayor Jacob proposed a comprehensive public transportation plan to reduce congestion. However, the factions couldn't agree on the plan due to fears of losing parking spaces or affecting local businesses. Jacob decided to hold town hall meetings, inviting local residents to share their experiences and concerns and used their collective wisdom to create a more inclusive solution.

Racial Tensions: Mayor Jacob understood that racial tensions were a significant barrier to unity in the city. He witnessed firsthand the fear and distrust between different ethnic groups, which led to incidents of violence and unrest. To address this, Jacob organised community-building events, such as multicultural festivals, and facilitated open dialogues between groups to foster understanding and empathy.

Gentrification: Mayor Jacob was concerned about the growing gentrification in the city, which was causing a deep divide between the wealthy newcomers and long-time residents. The fear of being displaced from their homes and neighbourhoods was palpable among the latter group. Jacob implemented affordable housing initiatives and supported local businesses, aiming to preserve the city's unique character and ensure that all residents felt secure in their community.

Environmental Concerns: The city faced pressing environmental issues, such as air pollution and waste management. Mayor Jacob proposed ambitious plans for a greener city. However, factions within the city council feared that these initiatives would be too costly or negatively impact businesses. To address these concerns, Jacob organised educational workshops and pilot programs, demonstrating the long-term benefits of sustainable practices and alleviating fears by showcasing the positive impact on both the environment and the local economy.

By addressing these daily challenges head-on, Mayor Jacob showed his constituents that it was possible to overcome their fears and insecurities by working together. His leadership style prioritised open communication, empathy, and collaboration, allowing him to unite the city's competing factions and create a more harmonious community. In doing so, Mayor Jacob offered his citizens a powerful example of how to navigate their daily lives by managing their fears and working together towards a common goal.

As he learns about the "Fear on Fire" movement, Mayor Jacob finds the inspiration to bring his city together and overcome the divisions that have held it back.

Embracing the principles of courage, resilience, and unity, Mayor Jacob embarks on a campaign to promote open dialogue, empathy, and collaboration among the city's residents. Through town hall meetings, public forums, and social initiatives, he encourages people to share their fears, listen to one another, and work together to find common ground.

As the city begins to heal and unite, the progress that once seemed impossible becomes achievable. New policies and initiatives are implemented, benefiting all residents and setting an example for other divided communities to follow.

Mayor Jacob's story highlights the transformative power of confronting fear in politics and the potential for unity and progress when leaders and citizens embrace the principles of the "Fear on Fire" movement. As the movement continues to spread, more communities are inspired to face their fears, bridge divides, and work together for a better future.

CHAPTER 33

THE COURAGEOUS WHISTLEBLOWER

In the world of politics, transparency and accountability were essential to maintaining the public's trust and promoting good governance. However, those who dared to expose corruption or wrongdoing often faced significant fears, including the fear of retribution, loss of employment, or threats to their personal safety. History is filled with examples that demonstrate the varying levels of corruption and the courage required to expose it.

Julius Caesar: Julius Caesar's rise to power in ancient Rome was marked by political intrigue and rampant corruption. Some politicians, like Cicero, dared to speak out against corruption, despite the fear of retribution from Caesar and his supporters. Unfortunately, Caesar's eventual assassination was a testament to the dangers faced by those who challenged the status quo.

Egyptian Pharaohs: Ancient Egypt's powerful rulers were notorious for corruption and exploitation. They amassed vast wealth, often at the expense of their subjects. Historians have uncovered evidence of individuals who risked their lives to expose the corruption within the Pharaoh's court, knowing that faced severe punishment if caught.

Persian Empire: Corruption was rampant within the Persian Empire, as officials and administrators embezzled funds and accepted bribes. There were brave whistleblowers who attempted to expose the corruption, but they often faced severe consequences, including exile, imprisonment, or execution.

Alexander the Great: Alexander the Great's vast empire was built on conquest and expansion, which inevitably led to corruption within his administration. As his empire grew, Alexander had to deal with numerous cases of bribery and embezzlement among his governors and officials. Those who reported corruption faced potential retribution from the powerful individuals they accused.

British Empire: The British Empire was known for its extensive bureaucracy and colonial administration, which provided ample opportunities for corruption. Throughout its history, brave individuals took on the establishment, risking their careers and personal safety to expose wrongdoing. One notable example is the impeachment of Warren Hastings, the first Governor-General of Bengal, on charges of corruption and abuse of power.

Adolf Hitler's Nazi Germany: In Nazi Germany, corruption was widespread, and those who dared to expose it faced severe consequences. The most famous example is the White Rose resistance group, which was led by university students who secretly distributed leaflets denouncing the Nazi regime. The group's members were arrested and executed for their actions.

Modern-day examples: Today, we see examples of corruption and the courage required to expose it in countries like Russia, Iran, North Korea, Myanmar, Saudi Arabia, India and some African Nations. Brave individuals and journalists risk their lives and careers to expose corruption, often facing threats to their personal safety and livelihoods.

These historical and modern-day examples demonstrate that corruption is an unfortunate part of human nature. However, they also show the remarkable courage of those who face their fears to expose wrongdoing and promote transparency and accountability. By shining a light on these brave individuals, we can inspire others to stand up against corruption and strive for a more just and equitable world.

The "Fear on Fire" movement recognised the importance of whistleblowers in holding the powerful accountable and encouraged them to confront their fears while standing up for truth and justice.

In this chapter, we follow the story of Elena, a government employee who uncovers a major corruption scandal within her department. Despite the risks, she is determined to bring the truth to light, but the fear of retaliation and the potential consequences for her family weigh heavily on her conscience. As she learns about the "Fear on Fire" movement, Elena, a young and idealistic civil servant, finds the courage to confront her fears and take a stand against corruption within her government. She realises that harnessing the power of fear, rather than being paralyzed by it, can give her the strength and determination to make a difference.

Understanding the nature of fear and learning to manage it is vital to Elena's journey. She begins to see that by channelling her fear into a burning passion for justice, she can ignite the fire within herself and those around her. This "Fear on Fire" momentum allows her to rally others to her cause, inspiring them to join her in fighting corruption.

Elena starts by gathering evidence of corruption within her department and using her network to bring attention to the issue. As her efforts gain traction, she faces numerous challenges and risks, including threats to her career and personal safety. Yet, fueled by her newfound understanding of fear, she remains steadfast and continues her fight.

The more Elena fights, the more she inspires others to join her cause. Her story spreads, and soon people from all walks of life are drawn to the movement. They too begin to confront their fears, using the power of the

"Fear on Fire" movement to drive change in their communities.

Elena's leadership and the collective consciousness of the people she has united create a powerful force against corruption. The momentum of the "Fear on Fire" movement becomes unstoppable, leading to significant reforms and greater transparency within the government. As the movement grows, it serves as a reminder that when individuals confront their fears and channel them into positive action, they can create meaningful change in the world.

As news of Elena's bravery spreads, the public demands greater transparency and accountability from their leaders, leading to widespread reforms that promote good governance and restore trust in the political system.

Elena's story demonstrates the power of confronting fear in the pursuit of truth and justice and the potential for positive change when individuals embrace the principles of the "Fear on Fire" movement. As the movement continues to spread, more people are inspired to face their fears, stand up for what is right, and work together to build a more just and accountable society.

CHAPTER 34

THE DIPLOMAT'S CHALLENGE

In an increasingly interconnected world, diplomacy played a crucial role in maintaining peace, fostering cooperation, and addressing global challenges. Diplomats and negotiators faced numerous fears in their line of work, such as the fear of escalating tensions, failing to reach agreements, or being perceived as weak by their counterparts. Let's explore some examples that demonstrate the importance of diplomacy and the stress diplomats face daily.

Cuban Missile Crisis: In 1962, the world was on the brink of nuclear war when the US discovered Soviet missiles in Cuba. Diplomats from both sides, including US President John F. Kennedy and Soviet Premier Nikita Khrushchev, had to navigate intense fear and pressure to reach a peaceful resolution, ultimately avoiding a devastating conflict.

Iran Nuclear Deal: The 2015 Iran Nuclear Deal, also known as the Joint Comprehensive Plan of Action (JCPOA), was a result of years of intense diplomatic efforts by multiple nations, including the US, Iran, and European countries. Diplomats faced immense pressure to strike a balance between ensuring Iran's nuclear program remained peaceful and addressing the concerns of sceptical nations, such as Israel and Saudi Arabia.

Paris Climate Agreement: Diplomats from 196 countries came together in 2015 to negotiate the Paris Climate Agreement, a landmark deal aimed at combating climate change. These negotiators had to navigate diverse interests, conflicting demands, and immense pressure from their home countries to create a global framework for reducing greenhouse gas emissions.

US-China Trade Negotiations: Diplomats from the US and China have been engaged in tense trade negotiations for years, attempting to resolve disputes while avoiding further escalation. These negotiators face significant stress as they work to balance the interests of their countries amidst a backdrop of economic competition and geopolitical rivalry.

North Korea Nuclear Negotiations: Diplomats from countries such as the US, South Korea, and Japan have been involved in delicate negotiations with North Korea to address its nuclear program. These negotiators face the constant fear of escalating tensions and potential conflict, as well as the pressure to reach a deal that ensures regional stability.

These examples illustrate the importance of diplomacy and the immense stress diplomats face daily. To succeed in their roles, diplomats must possess a deep understanding of the issues at hand, the ability to navigate complex relationships, and the capacity to manage their fears. Embracing the principles of "Fear on Fire" and developing the clarity that comes from a calm and focused mind can be invaluable in helping diplomats make sound decisions and navigate the high-stakes world of international diplomacy.

The "Fear on Fire" movement recognized the unique challenges faced by diplomats and encouraged them to confront their fears while working towards peaceful, collaborative solutions that benefited all parties involved.

In this chapter, we follow the story of Ambassador Amina, a seasoned diplomat tasked with resolving a high-stakes conflict between two nations on the brink of war. Fear permeates every aspect of the negotiations, with both sides unwilling to make concessions due to concerns about national pride, security, and potential backlash.

As Amina learns about the "Fear on Fire" movement, she finds the courage to confront her own fears and develops a creative, bold approach to the negotiations, aimed at fostering trust and breaking down barriers between the two nations.

Embracing the principles of courage, resilience, and unity, Ambassador Amina encourages both sides to engage in honest, open dialogue, share their fears and concerns, and focus on the long-term benefits of cooperation and peace. Through her tireless efforts, she manages to broker an agreement that not only prevents war but also paves the way for future collaboration and understanding between the nations.

Amina's story highlights the transformative power of confronting fear in diplomacy and the potential for peaceful, cooperative solutions when diplomats embrace the principles of the "Fear on Fire" movement.

CHAPTER 35

THE POWER OF THE GRASSROOT MOVEMENTS

In the realm of politics, grassroots movements and civic engagement were essential to driving change and holding leaders accountable. However, organisers and activists often faced fears related to public backlash, personal safety, or the potential failure of their campaigns.

The "Fear on Fire" movement acknowledged the importance of grassroots activism and encouraged organisers to confront their fears while working to create positive change in their communities and beyond.

In this chapter, we follow the story of Carlos, a community organiser who is passionate about addressing social inequality in his neighbourhood. He dreams of launching a grassroots campaign to push for policy changes, but the fear of failure and the possibility of facing opposition from powerful interest groups hold him back. As Carlos learns about the "Fear on Fire" movement, he finds the courage to confront his fears and take action.

Guided by the principles of courage, resilience, and unity, Carlos rallies his community to join him in the fight for social justice. Through door-to-door campaigning, social media engagement, and organised events, they raise awareness about the issues facing their community and build momentum for change.

As the movement gains traction, Carlos and his fellow activists successfully pressure local politicians to address their concerns, leading to the implementation of new policies aimed at reducing inequality and improving the lives of the community's residents.

Carlos's story demonstrates the power of confronting fear in grassroots activism and the potential for positive change when ordinary citizens embrace the principles of the "Fear on Fire" movement. As the movement continues to spread, more people are inspired to face their fears, engage in civic action, and work together to build a more just and equitable society.

CHAPTER 36

THE RISE OF FEARLESS LEADERS

In a world where fear dictated the lives of many, the "Fear on Fire" movement began to inspire a new generation of political leaders who were unafraid to tackle complex issues, challenge the status quo, and embrace the principles of courage, resilience, and unity.

In this chapter, we follow the story of Maya, a young, passionate activist who is inspired by the "Fear on Fire" movement to pursue a career in politics. Despite the fear of public scrutiny, potential failure, or facing opposition from entrenched political forces, she decides to run for public office, determined to make a difference in her community.

Guided by the principles of the "Fear on Fire" movement, Maya builds a diverse, inclusive campaign team that reflects the values she wishes to bring to her community. They focus on addressing long-standing issues, such as education, healthcare, and environmental sustainability, while also promoting open dialogue and civic engagement.

As Maya's campaign gains momentum, her message resonates with voters who are tired of fear-driven politics and yearn for positive change. Her authenticity and commitment to the values of the "Fear on Fire" movement helped her win the election and become a trailblazer in her community.

Once in office, Maya works tirelessly to implement policies that align with the "Fear on Fire" movement's principles and bring about lasting change in her community. Her leadership serves as an inspiration to others, and soon, more fearless leaders emerge to champion the movement's cause across the nation.

Maya's story highlights the transformative power of confronting fear in politics and the potential for progress when new leaders embrace the principles of the "Fear on Fire" movement. As the movement continues to spread, more individuals are inspired to face their fears, take on leadership roles, and work together to create a brighter future for all

CHAPTER 37

FEAR AND THE MEDIA

In a world dominated by fear, the role of the media in shaping public opinion and driving political discourse was more critical than ever. Journalists and media outlets often faced fears of their own, such as pressure from powerful interests, threats to their safety, or the fear of losing credibility.

The "Fear on Fire" movement recognized the vital role that the media played in promoting transparency, accountability, and informed discourse, and encouraged journalists to confront their fears while upholding the highest standards of integrity and professionalism.

In this chapter, we follow the story of Aditi, an investigative journalist who is determined to expose corruption and abuse of power, despite the fear of reprisals from those she investigates. As she learns about the "Fear on Fire" movement, Aditi finds the courage to confront her fears and pursue her mission to reveal the truth, no matter the cost.

Guided by the principles of courage, resilience, and unity, Aditi delves into a high-profile case that uncovers a web of deceit and corruption at the highest levels of government. Her fearless reporting exposes the truth, leading to significant reforms and inspiring other journalists to take on similar stories.

As the media begins to embrace the "Fear on Fire" movement, journalists and media outlets prioritise honest, unbiased reporting over sensationalism and fear-mongering. This shift in focus leads to a more informed public, empowering citizens to engage in meaningful political discussions and hold their leaders accountable.

Aditi's story demonstrates the power of confronting fear in journalism and the potential for positive change when media professionals embrace the principles of the "Fear on Fire" movement.

CHAPTER 38

EDUCATION AS A CATALYST FOR CHANGE

In a world riddled with fear, education played a crucial role in empowering individuals to confront their fears and develop the skills needed to bring about change in their lives and communities. Sadly, there were many countries that lagged behind in education, still teaching outdated curricula that perpetuated old ideologies and colonial perspectives.

One glaring example of this lack of foresight was the slow adoption of the English language in many European countries. Despite the widespread use of English for international business and trade, some countries resisted promoting or learning it, leaving them struggling to catch up in the 21st century.

To bring about meaningful change, it was essential for countries to invest in updating their education systems, keeping them relevant to the current global landscape. This would entail not only revising curricula but also addressing the political and social barriers that hindered progress. In many cases, the reluctance to bring about change stemmed from two key factors: the cost and time involved in overhauling the education system, and the desire of old-school politicians to maintain control by keeping the population uninformed and mired in outdated ideas.

Advocates for education reform, inspired by the "Fear on Fire" movement, understood that grassroots education played a vital role in transforming societies. They recognized that confronting the fear of change and working tirelessly to break down barriers would ultimately lead to a brighter, more informed future for all. The "Fear on Fire" movement recognized the importance of education in fostering resilience, critical thinking, and empathy, and encouraged educators to confront their fears while inspiring students to do the same.

In this chapter, we follow the story of Mr Thompson, a dedicated teacher who is passionate about empowering his students to overcome fear and become agents of change. Despite the fear of pushback from traditionalists or potential backlash from parents, he decides to incorporate the principles of the "Fear on Fire" movement into his teaching.

Guided by the principles of courage, resilience, and unity, Mr Thompson develops an innovative curriculum that encourages students to engage in open dialogue, embrace diverse perspectives, and tackle challenging issues. Through project-based learning, collaborative problem-solving, and the exploration of global issues, students learn to confront their fears and develop the skills needed to bring about positive change.

As word of Mr Thompson's transformative teaching methods spreads, other educators become inspired to adopt the "Fear on Fire" principles in their classrooms. This shift in educational focus leads to a generation of young people who are better equipped to address the challenges of a fear-driven world and work together to create a brighter future.

CHAPTER 39

FEAR AND MENTAL HEALTH

In a world where fear was a constant presence, the impact on mental health was undeniable. Anxiety, depression, and other mental health issues were exacerbated by the pervasive nature of fear, affecting the lives of countless individuals. Sarah, who had struggled with her own mental health challenges, found a way to overcome fear and improve her well-being.

Sarah began her journey by acknowledging her fears and seeking professional help. She attended therapy sessions and learned various coping techniques to help her manage her anxiety and depression. Additionally, she started practising mindfulness and meditation to help her stay present and focused on the moment, reducing the power of fear over her thoughts.

One day-to-day example of Sarah overcoming her fear was when she had to give a presentation at work. In the past, her fear of public speaking would have caused her to panic, but she decided to apply what she had learned. She took deep breaths to calm her nerves, visualised a successful outcome, and reminded herself of her past accomplishments. By doing so, she was able to deliver the presentation with confidence.

Another example was when Sarah faced financial difficulties. Instead of giving in to fear and worry, she took control of the situation by seeking advice from a financial advisor, creating a budget, and finding ways to increase her income. These practical steps helped her to regain her sense of control and reduce her anxiety about the future.

These real-time examples demonstrated how Sarah was able to use the techniques she learned in therapy and through mindfulness practices to manage her mental health issues. By confronting her fears head-on and taking proactive steps to address them, she gradually regained control over her life and improved her overall well-being.

Readers facing similar challenges can take inspiration from Sarah's story and consider seeking professional help, practising mindfulness and meditation, and adopting practical coping strategies to manage their fears and improve their mental health.

In this chapter, we follow the story of Sarah, a young woman struggling with anxiety and depression, as she grapples with the fear of judgement and the stigma associated with mental health. As Sarah learns about the "Fear on Fire" movement, she finds the courage to confront her fears and seek help for her mental health challenges.

Guided by the principles of courage, resilience, and unity, Sarah begins attending therapy and support groups, where she meets others who are experiencing similar challenges. Through shared experiences and mutual support, they learn to face their fears, develop coping strategies, and work towards improved mental health.

As Sarah's journey progresses, she becomes an advocate for mental health awareness and starts a local "Fear on Fire" support group to help others in her community facing similar challenges. Her efforts contribute to a growing awareness of the importance of mental health and the need for accessible resources and support.

Sarah's story highlights the transformative power of confronting fear in the realm of mental health and the potential for positive change when individuals embrace the principles of the "Fear on Fire" movement. As the movement continues to spread, more people are inspired to face their fears, seek help, and work together to build a more compassionate and understanding society.

CHAPTER 40

FEAR AND THE ENVIRONMENT

In a world where fear was pervasive, the urgent need to address environmental challenges and protect the planet was often overshadowed by short-term concerns and political agendas. The "Fear on Fire" movement recognized the importance of confronting fear in order to tackle environmental issues and encouraged individuals, organisations, and governments to take bold action.

In this chapter, we follow the story of Dr Kim, an environmental scientist who is passionate about finding solutions to the pressing issue of climate change. Despite the fear of backlash from powerful interest groups or the uncertainty surrounding the success of her research, Dr Kim decides to confront her fears and devote her life to environmental activism and research.

Guided by the principles of courage, resilience, and unity, Dr Kim leads a team of scientists and activists in developing innovative solutions to mitigate the impacts of climate change and promote sustainable practices. Through collaboration with other researchers, policymakers, and industry leaders, they work together to implement real, lasting change.

As Dr Kim's work gains recognition, she becomes an influential voice in the global fight against climate change, inspiring others to confront their fears and join the cause. The "Fear on Fire" movement gains momentum in the environmental sphere, leading to a global shift in attitudes and actions to protect the planet.

Dr Kim's story highlights the transformative power of confronting fear in addressing environmental challenges and the potential for positive change when individuals and organisations embrace the principles of the "Fear on Fire" movement. As the movement continues to spread, more people are inspired to face their fears, take action, and work together to build a sustainable future for all.

CHAPTER 41

THE DOUBLE-EDGED SWORD OF SCIENTIFIC PROGRESS

In a world where fear was a driving force, the impact on science and technology was significant. The "Fear on Fire" movement recognized that fear could both motivate and hinder scientific progress, leading to a complex interplay between the desire for discovery and the potential consequences of new technologies.

In this chapter, we examine the impact of fear on scientific research and technological advancements, particularly in the context of the global arms race. The ongoing conflict in Ukraine and rising tensions among various nations have led to a renewed emphasis on military technology and the race to develop increasingly powerful and sophisticated weaponry.

As countries like the UK, France, China, Australia, Japan, South Korea, the Philippines, North Korea, India, Germany, and other European nations invest heavily in upgrading their arsenals, the pressure on scientists and engineers to develop new technologies is immense. The fear of falling behind in the arms race or the potential for new technologies to be used against their own nation drives researchers to push the boundaries of what is possible.

However, the "Fear on Fire" movement highlights the importance of confronting these fears and considering the broader implications of scientific and technological advancements. It encourages scientists, engineers, and policymakers to consider the potential consequences of their work, striving for innovations that benefit humanity rather than perpetuating fear and conflict.

Dr Patel, a brilliant scientist working on cutting-edge military technology, found himself grappling with the fear of contributing to a destructive arms race. As he became increasingly aware of the potential consequences of his work, he realised the need for a peaceful solution.

Driven by his conviction that there must be a better way, Dr Patel began to explore alternative applications of his research. He shifted his focus from developing destructive weapons to creating technologies that could be used for humanitarian and peacekeeping purposes. He reached out to colleagues, both within his own country and internationally, to foster collaboration and exchange ideas.

One of Dr Patel's most significant achievements was the development of cutting-edge drone technology that could be used for disaster relief and search and rescue operations. This technology proved invaluable in saving lives during natural disasters and other emergencies, earning Dr Patel recognition and support from his peers and the public alike.

Despite the ongoing tensions and arms race, Dr Patel managed to bring together experts from various countries to form a global network of scientists and engineers dedicated to promoting peace and humanitarian efforts. This coalition worked tirelessly to develop innovative technologies that could be used to address global challenges and alleviate human suffering, rather than perpetuating violence and destruction.

Through conferences, workshops, and joint research initiatives, Dr Patel's coalition inspired a new generation of scientists to embrace the potential of their work for good. In doing so, they shifted the focus from an arms race to a race for peace, progress, and the betterment of humanity.

Dr Patel's story serves as a powerful reminder that the pursuit of peace and collaboration is not only possible but essential in a world riddled with fear and conflict. It is through the efforts of individuals like Dr Patel that we can begin to imagine a brighter, more peaceful future for all.

Inspired by the "Fear on Fire" movement, he confronts his fears and begins to explore alternative applications for his research that could contribute to global peace and stability.

Dr Patel's story demonstrates the importance of confronting fear in the realm of science and technology and highlights the potential for positive change when researchers and policymakers embrace the principles of the "Fear on Fire" movement. As the movement continues to spread, more people are inspired to face their fears, critically assess the implications of their work, and strive for a more collaborative and peaceful future.

CHAPTER 42

THE ETHICAL DILEMMA OF ADVANCING TECHNOLOGIES

In a world driven by fear, the rapid pace of technological innovation presented both opportunities and challenges. The "Fear on Fire" movement emphasised the need for ethical considerations in the development and implementation of new technologies, encouraging scientists, engineers, and policymakers to confront their fears and make responsible choices.

In this chapter, we delve into the ethical dilemmas faced by those working at the forefront of science and technology. We explore the balance between the pursuit of scientific advancement and the potential consequences of these advancements, particularly in the context of surveillance, artificial intelligence, and biotechnology.

We follow the story of Dr Lee, an AI researcher grappling with the implications of her work on autonomous weapons systems. As the "Fear on Fire," movement gains traction, she becomes increasingly concerned about the potential for her research to be used in ways that amplify fear and escalate the conflict.

Inspired by the principles of courage, resilience, and unity, Dr Lee confronts her fears and decides to pivot her research toward developing AI technologies that promote peace, cooperation, and global understanding. Alongside other like-minded scientists, she advocates for ethical guidelines and regulatory frameworks that ensure new technologies are developed and deployed responsibly.

As Dr Lee's work gains recognition, the "Fear on Fire" movement encourages more researchers to consider the ethical implications of their work, leading to a growing movement for responsible innovation in science and technology. This shift helps to mitigate some of the potential negative consequences of rapid technological advancements and focuses on harnessing technology for the greater good.

Dr Lee's story highlights the importance of confronting fear in the realm of science and technology and demonstrates the potential for positive change when researchers and policymakers embrace the principles of the "Fear on Fire" movement. As the movement continues to spread, more people are inspired to face their fears, critically assess the implications of their work, and strive to develop technologies that benefit humanity rather than exacerbate fear and conflict.

CHAPTER 43

BRIDGING THE DIGITAL DIVIDE

In a world where fear was pervasive, the digital divide between those with access to advanced technologies and those without became a significant source of concern. The "Fear on Fire" movement recognized that addressing this inequality was essential for creating a more unified and resilient global community.

In this chapter, we follow the story of Maria, a social entrepreneur who is passionate about using technology to empower disadvantaged communities. Despite the fear of failure or the challenges of working in resource-limited settings, Maria confronts her fears and launches a bold initiative aimed at bridging the digital divide.

Guided by the principles of courage, resilience, and unity, Maria and her team work tirelessly to bring affordable internet access, digital literacy programs, and cutting-edge educational resources to underprivileged communities around the world. Through partnerships with tech companies, governments, and NGOs, they help to level the playing field and provide new opportunities for those who have been left behind by the digital revolution.

As word of Maria's initiative spreads, more people become inspired to join the "Fear on Fire" movement and confront their fears in the pursuit of a more equitable and connected world. The movement sparks a global conversation about the need for inclusive and accessible technology, leading to significant investments in digital infrastructure and educational initiatives that help bridge the digital divide.

Maria's story demonstrates the transformative power of confronting fear in the realm of technology and highlights the potential for positive change when individuals and organisations embrace the principles of the "Fear on Fire" movement. As the movement continues to spread, more people are inspired to face their fears, pursue innovative solutions, and work together to build a more connected and inclusive global community.

CHAPTER 44

THE FEAR OF TECHNOLOGICAL UNEMPLOYMENT

In a world dominated by fear, technological unemployment emerged as a significant concern. Rapid advancements in automation, artificial intelligence, and robotics led to a growing anxiety about job displacement and the uncertain future of work. The "Fear on Fire" movement recognised the importance of addressing this fear and finding innovative solutions to adapt to the changing landscape of employment.

Governments around the world can address the issue of growing unemployment through various strategies and initiatives:

Emphasising education and lifelong learning: Governments should invest in education and training programs that equip individuals with the skills needed to adapt to the changing job market. This includes offering courses in emerging fields like data science, machine learning, and renewable energy, as well as promoting lifelong learning opportunities for adults to upskill and reskill.

Encouraging entrepreneurship and innovation: Governments can promote entrepreneurship and innovation by providing financial incentives, mentoring, and support for startups and small businesses. This will help create new job opportunities, drive economic growth, and foster a culture of innovation.

Supporting the transition to new industries: As traditional industries become obsolete, governments can help workers transition to new industries by providing targeted training programs, financial assistance, and job placement services.

Implementing social safety nets: Governments should strengthen social safety nets to support workers who are displaced by technological advancements. This can include providing unemployment benefits, healthcare, and affordable housing, as well as implementing policies that promote job sharing or shortened work weeks.

Promoting collaboration between industry and education: Governments can foster partnerships between educational institutions and industries to ensure that curricula are aligned with the skills required in the job market. This will help bridge the gap between education and employment and better prepare students for the future of work.

Encouraging remote work and flexible employment: Governments can promote remote work and flexible employment opportunities by creating the necessary infrastructure and adopting policies that support these work arrangements. This can help workers adapt to the changing nature of work while also improving work-life balance.

By taking these steps, governments can help mitigate the fear of technological unemployment and ensure that workers are better prepared for the rapidly evolving job market. Addressing this fear will require a multifaceted approach that focuses on education, innovation, and social support, ultimately empowering individuals to embrace change and thrive in the face of uncertainty.

In this chapter, we follow the story of Alex, a labour union leader, who is determined to protect the interests of workers in the face of growing automation. Alex confronts the fear of technological unemployment by advocating for better training, education, and support for workers in industries most affected by automation.

Guided by the principles of courage, resilience, and unity, Alex works with employers, governments, and educational institutions to develop comprehensive retraining programs and new career pathways for displaced workers. These programs focus on fostering skills that are in high demand and less susceptible to automation, such as creativity, critical thinking, and emotional intelligence.

As Alex's efforts gain momentum, the "Fear on Fire" movement spreads among workers and organisations alike, inspiring a broader conversation about the future of work and the need for a more adaptive and resilient workforce. This shift leads to increased investment in education, retraining initiatives, and innovative policies that promote job security and sustainable employment in the age of automation.

CHAPTER 45

ENCOURAGING RESPONSIBLE TECHNOLOGICAL INNOVATION

In a world filled with fear, the rapid pace of technological innovation often created a sense of uncertainty and apprehension. The "Fear on Fire" movement emphasised the importance of responsible innovation and encouraged scientists, engineers, and policymakers to confront their fears while developing new technologies that benefit society as a whole.

In this chapter, we follow the story of Dr Thompson, a leading biotechnology researcher who is committed to developing responsible and ethical solutions to global health challenges. Faced with the fear of unintended consequences and the potential misuse of his research, Dr Thompson grapples with the complex ethical landscape surrounding his work.

Guided by the principles of courage, resilience, and unity, Dr Thompson collaborates with other researchers, ethicists, and policymakers to develop a set of guidelines and best practices for responsible innovation in biotechnology. Their collective efforts aim to ensure that new technologies are developed with a focus on safety, transparency, and long-term societal impact.

As Dr Thompson's work gains recognition, the "Fear on Fire" movement encourages more researchers and organisations to prioritise responsible innovation, fostering a culture of collaboration and accountability in the scientific community. This shift leads to the development of groundbreaking biotechnologies that are carefully designed to improve global health while minimising potential risks and unintended consequences.

Dr Thompson's story highlights the importance of confronting fear in the realm of science and technology and demonstrates the potential for positive change when individuals and organisations embrace the principles of the "Fear on Fire" movement. As the movement continues to spread, more people are inspired to face their fears, promote responsible innovation, and work together to develop transformative technologies that benefit humanity and our planet.

CHAPTER 46

THE POWER OF COLLABORATION

In a world fuelled by fear, the potential for transformative change often lay dormant, stifled by apprehension and uncertainty. The "Fear on Fire" movement recognized the importance of collaboration in overcoming fear and unlocking the full potential of technological advancements for the betterment of society.

In this chapter, we follow the story of Lila, a young entrepreneur who is passionate about harnessing technology to address global challenges, such as climate change and inequality. Faced with the fear of failure and the enormity of the problems she seeks to address, Lila realises that the key to overcoming these obstacles lies in fostering collaboration across disciplines, industries, and borders.

Guided by the principles of courage, resilience, and unity, Lila establishes a global network of researchers, engineers, entrepreneurs, and policymakers committed to working together in pursuit of innovative solutions to pressing global issues. By breaking down silos and encouraging the sharing of knowledge, resources, and expertise, Lila's network accelerates the development and implementation of groundbreaking technologies that have a positive impact on the world.

As Lila's collaborative network gains recognition, the "Fear on Fire" movement inspires more people to embrace the power of collaboration and confront their fears together. This shift leads to a surge in joint ventures, research partnerships, and cross-disciplinary initiatives that drive technological innovation and address pressing global challenges more effectively.

Lila's story highlights the importance of collaboration in overcoming fear and demonstrates the potential for positive change when individuals and organisations embrace the principles of the "Fear on Fire" movement. As the movement continues to spread, more people are inspired to face their fears, work together, and harness the power of technology to create a better future for all.

CHAPTER 47

FOSTERING A CULTURE OF TRUST

In a world gripped by fear, trust was a rare and valuable commodity. The "Fear on Fire" movement recognized that cultivating trust between individuals, organisations, and nations was essential for overcoming fear and unlocking the full potential of technological advancements.

In this chapter, we follow the story of Amina, a diplomat who works tirelessly to build bridges between nations and foster a culture of trust in a fearful world. Confronted with the challenges of navigating complex political landscapes and deep-seated mistrust, Amina remains steadfast in her commitment to promoting dialogue, cooperation, and mutual understanding.

Guided by the principles of courage, resilience, and unity, Amina works to establish diplomatic channels and forums that enable countries to come together and share their experiences, knowledge, and resources in the pursuit of collaborative solutions to global challenges. By fostering trust and promoting transparency, Amina's efforts help to ease tensions, diffuse conflicts, and create an environment where technological innovations can be shared for the greater good.

As Amina's diplomatic initiatives gain recognition, the "Fear on Fire" movement inspires more people to embrace the importance of trust and to work together to overcome fear. This shift leads to increased international cooperation, joint research projects, and the formation of global alliances that harness technology to address pressing issues such as climate change, poverty, and inequality.

Amina's story highlights the importance of trust in overcoming fear and demonstrates the potential for positive change when individuals and nations embrace the principles of the "Fear on Fire" movement. As the movement continues to spread, more people are inspired to face their fears, cultivate trust, and work together to create a more connected, cooperative, and peaceful world.

CHAPTER 48

THE ROLE OF EDUCATION

In a world plagued by fear, education played a vital role in empowering individuals to confront their fears and embrace a brighter future. The "Fear on Fire" movement recognized the transformative power of education in shaping the minds and hearts of future generations and fostering resilience in the face of adversity.

In this chapter, we follow the story of Maya, an educator who is passionate about equipping students with the skills and knowledge necessary to navigate a rapidly changing world. Facing the challenge of preparing her students for an uncertain future, Maya endeavours to cultivate a learning environment that nurtures courage, resilience, and unity.

Guided by the principles of the "Fear on Fire" movement, Maya develops an innovative curriculum that goes beyond traditional subjects and emphasises critical thinking, creativity, empathy, and adaptability. By incorporating real-world issues and encouraging students to confront their fears, Maya's educational approach inspires young minds to become agents of change in their communities and the world at large.

As word of Maya's educational initiatives spreads, the "Fear on Fire" movement gains momentum in schools and educational institutions across the globe. This shift leads to a renewed focus on holistic education, which empowers students to confront their fears and embrace the challenges and opportunities of a rapidly changing world.

Maya's story highlights the crucial role of education in overcoming fear and demonstrates the potential for positive change when educators and institutions embrace the principles of the "Fear on Fire" movement. As the movement continues to spread, more people are inspired to face their fears, invest in education, and work together to create a more resilient and fearless future for all.

CHAPTER 49

HARNESSING THE POWER OF ART AND CREATIVITY

In a world consumed by fear, the power of art and creativity offered a vital means of expression, healing, and inspiration. The "Fear on Fire" movement recognized the role of artists in challenging fear and encouraging individuals to embrace courage, resilience, and unity.

In this chapter, we follow the story of Leila, a talented artist who uses her creative talents to explore the complexities of fear and inspire others to confront their own fears. Through her art, Leila seeks to spark meaningful conversations, challenge societal norms, and promote empathy and understanding.

Guided by the principles of the "Fear on Fire" movement, Leila creates a series of powerful art installations, performances, and interactive experiences that engage audiences and encourage them to face their fears. These artistic expressions resonate deeply with people from all walks of life, inspiring them to question their own fears and consider the possibilities of a world free from fear.

As Leila's art gains recognition, the "Fear on Fire" movement spreads throughout the creative community, leading to a flourishing of artistic expressions that address fear, courage, and resilience. This creative renaissance fosters a global conversation about the power of art to transform fear and challenges individuals to harness their own creativity to confront their fears and build a more fearless future.

Leila's story highlights the importance of art and creativity in overcoming fear and demonstrates the potential for positive change when artists and creatives embrace the principles of the "Fear on Fire" movement. As the movement continues to spread, more people are inspired to face their fears, engage with art, and work together to create a more courageous, resilient, and united world.

CHAPTER 50

A FEARLESS FUTURE

The Global Impact of the "Fear on Fire" Movement

As the "Fear on Fire" movement gains momentum across the globe, the world begins to witness a remarkable transformation. The movement's principles of courage, resilience, and unity have inspired countless individuals to confront their fears, leading to profound changes in personal lives, communities, and nations.

In this chapter, we take a step back and observe the global impact of the "Fear on Fire" movement. As the stories of individuals like Alex, Dr Thompson, Lila, Amina, Maya, and Leila continue to unfold, their influence spreads far and wide, creating a ripple effect of positive change that transcends borders and touches the lives of millions.

Through international collaboration, countries unite in their efforts to address pressing global challenges such as climate change, poverty, and inequality. The power of trust and cooperation leads to the development of innovative solutions that benefit humanity as a whole, fostering a more interconnected and supportive global community.

In the realms of science, technology, education, and art, the "Fear on Fire" movement encourages the pursuit of responsible innovation, the cultivation of adaptable and resilient workforces, and the exploration of creative outlets that challenge societal fears and inspire change.

As the world begins to shed the shackles of fear, a new era of hope, collaboration, and progress emerges. The global impact of the "Fear on Fire" movement serves as a powerful reminder of the potential that resides within each individual when they confront their fears and embrace the principles of courage, resilience, and unity.

The stories of the individuals who have been a part of this movement illustrate the extraordinary power of facing one's fears and the profound changes that can occur when people come together with a shared vision. As the "Fear on Fire," movement continues to spread, it paves the way for a brighter, more fearless future for all.

CHAPTER 51

THE FEAR FACTORY

The Role of Media in Amplifying Fear

In a world where fear permeates every aspect of life, the role of media in amplifying and perpetuating fear cannot be understated. The "Fear on Fire" movement recognizes the media's influence in shaping public opinion and strives to bring awareness to the ways in which fear is exploited to drive ratings, clicks, and shares.

In this chapter, we follow the story of Jackson, an investigative journalist determined to expose the inner workings of the media's "fear factory." Jackson's journey takes him behind the scenes of sensational news stories and fear-mongering headlines, revealing the mechanisms that drive the media's relentless focus on fear.

Guided by the principles of the "Fear on Fire" movement, Jackson works tirelessly to challenge the media's fear-based narratives and promote responsible journalism that prioritises accuracy, context, and nuance. Through his work, Jackson unveils the media's role in perpetuating fear, fuelling division, and exacerbating societal tensions.

As Jackson's findings gain attention, the "Fear on Fire" movement inspires a shift in media consumption habits, with more people seeking out balanced, responsible news sources that provide objective information without resorting to fear-mongering tactics. This change leads to a growing demand for ethical journalism, prompting media outlets to reevaluate their approaches to news reporting.

Jackson's story highlights the importance of confronting fear in the realm of media and demonstrates the potential for positive change when individuals and organisations embrace the principles of the "Fear on Fire" movement. As the movement continues to spread, more people are inspired to question the fear-based narratives that pervade the media and work together to promote responsible journalism that fosters understanding, empathy, and unity.

CHAPTER 52

THE RISE OF THE FEARLESS JOURNALISM

In a world where the media often feeds off fear, the "Fear on Fire" movement inspires a new wave of fearless journalism. This chapter focuses on a group of intrepid journalists and content creators who, inspired by Jackson's work, strive to create media that informs, educates, and unites people rather than stoking fear and division.

Together, they launch a new media outlet called "The Fearless Times," which is dedicated to reporting news stories with accuracy, context, and empathy. The Fearless Times prioritises in-depth analysis, investigative journalism, and constructive debates, while actively avoiding sensationalism and fear-mongering.

Guided by the principles of the "Fear on Fire" movement, the journalists at The Fearless Times work tirelessly to provide their audience with reliable information that empowers them to make informed decisions and confront their fears. They also create content that showcases inspiring stories of individuals who have faced their fears and made a difference in their communities.

As The Fearless Times gains recognition and support, its impact reverberates throughout the media industry. More media outlets start to adopt the principles of fearless journalism, leading to a shift in the news landscape that promotes understanding, empathy, and unity instead of fear and division.

The story of The Fearless Times demonstrates the power of ethical journalism in countering fear and exemplifies the positive change that can occur when media outlets embrace the principles of the "Fear on Fire" movement. As the movement continues to spread, more people are inspired to seek out and support fearless journalism, fostering a more informed, resilient, and united society.

CHAPTER 53

SOCIAL MEDIA AND THE FEAR PANDEMIC

In the digital age, social media plays an undeniable role in shaping public opinion and the ways in which information is disseminated. Unfortunately, social media platforms have also become breeding grounds for fear, amplifying anxiety and negative emotions that ripple throughout society.

In this chapter, we follow the story of Nina, a social media influencer who becomes increasingly disillusioned with the online world's obsession with fear and negativity. Nina recognizes that her platform has the potential to make a positive impact, and she becomes determined to use her influence to change the way people engage with social media.

Inspired by the "Fear on Fire" movement, Nina begins to create and share content that encourages her followers to confront their fears, embrace resilience, and support one another. Nina uses her platform to challenge sensationalist headlines, combat misinformation, and promote positive, constructive conversations.

As Nina's message of hope and unity gains traction, more influencers and content creators join her in the mission to combat fear on social media. Together, they form a network of individuals who are dedicated to creating a more supportive and empathetic online environment.

The story of Nina and her fellow influencers demonstrates the power of social media in overcoming fear and showcases the potential for positive change when individuals use their platforms responsibly. As the "Fear on Fire" movement continues to spread, more people are inspired to question the fear-based narratives that dominate social media and work together to create a more resilient, empathetic, and united digital world.

CHAPTER 54

MEDIA LITERACY AND EMPOWERING THE PUBLIC

In a world saturated with information, the ability to discern reliable sources from misleading or fear-inducing content becomes more crucial than ever. The "Fear on Fire" movement recognizes the importance of media literacy in enabling individuals to navigate the digital landscape with confidence and make informed decisions.

In this chapter, we follow the story of Sam, an educator who is passionate about teaching media literacy skills to people of all ages. Sam develops workshops and resources to help participants understand the inner workings of the media, recognize manipulation tactics, and critically evaluate the information they encounter online.

Guided by the principles of the "Fear on Fire" movement, Sam's media literacy programs empower participants to confront their fears by providing them with the tools they need to make sense of the complex media landscape. The programs emphasise the importance of consuming a balanced and diverse range of news sources, as well as fostering open-mindedness and healthy scepticism when engaging with online content.

As Sam's media literacy programs gain popularity, the "Fear on Fire" movement begins to permeate schools, universities, and community centres, leading to a widespread effort to promote media literacy and critical thinking skills. This educational shift equips individuals to resist fear-based narratives and make more informed decisions in their personal and professional lives.

Sam's story highlights the importance of media literacy in overcoming fear and demonstrates the potential for positive change when educators and institutions embrace the principles of the "Fear on Fire" movement. As the movement continues to spread, more people are inspired to develop their media literacy skills, fostering a more informed, resilient, and united society.

CHAPTER 55

THE TRANSFORMATION OF ADVERTISING

In a world driven by fear, advertising has long been an industry that capitalises on people's insecurities, anxieties, and concerns to sell products and services. However, as the "Fear on Fire," movement gains momentum, the advertising industry finds itself at a crossroads, compelled to re-evaluate its tactics and strategies.

In this chapter, we meet Emma, a creative director at a leading advertising agency, who becomes inspired by the "Fear on Fire" movement to transform the way her agency approaches advertising. Emma recognizes the power of advertising in shaping societal values and influencing consumer behaviour and becomes determined to create ad campaigns that empower and uplift rather than exploit fear.

Emma leads her team to develop innovative campaigns that focus on promoting positive messages, highlighting the strength and resilience of individuals, and encouraging consumers to confront their fears. These campaigns emphasise the importance of collaboration, empathy, and unity, reflecting the core principles of the "Fear on Fire" movement.

As Emma's agency gains recognition for its groundbreaking work, other advertising agencies begin to follow suit, leading to a transformation of the advertising industry. The shift toward empowering, fear-free advertising not only impacts the way consumers perceive products and services but also fosters a more resilient, confident, and united society.

Emma's story demonstrates the potential for positive change when advertising professionals embrace the principles of the "Fear on Fire" movement. As the movement continues to spread, more people within the industry are inspired to confront fear-based tactics and work together to create advertising that empowers, uplifts, and unites.

CHAPTER 56

ENTERTAINMENT

Overcoming Fear Through Stories

Entertainment has always played a crucial role in shaping public opinion and reflecting societal values. As the "Fear on Fire," movement gains traction, its influence begins to be felt in the world of entertainment, inspiring writers, filmmakers, and artists to create stories that challenge fear-based narratives and promote resilience, courage, and unity.

In this chapter, we meet Amir, a screenwriter who becomes inspired by the "Fear on Fire" movement to create a television series that tackles the theme of fear head-on. The show, titled "Fearless," follows a diverse group of characters as they confront their fears and overcome adversity, weaving together storylines that showcase the power of human resilience and the importance of empathy and cooperation.

As "Fearless" gains a dedicated following, its impact extends beyond the screen, inspiring conversations about fear, resilience, and unity in everyday life. Fans of the show create online communities where they share their personal experiences of confronting fear and support one another in their journeys toward a more fearless existence.

The success of "Fearless" signals a shift in the entertainment industry, with more creators embracing the principles of the "Fear on Fire" movement to tell stories that challenge fear and promote positive change. This transformation contributes to a cultural shift, fostering a more resilient, empathetic, and united society.

Amir's story highlights the power of entertainment in overcoming fear and illustrates the potential for positive change when artists and creators embrace the principles of the "Fear on Fire" movement. As the movement continues to spread, more people within the entertainment industry are inspired to create stories that empower, uplift, and unite, contributing to a more fearless and resilient world.

CHAPTER 57

THE POWER OF SPORTS

Uniting People Beyond Fear

In a world dominated by fear, sports have always served as a unifying force, transcending boundaries and bringing people together. The "Fear on Fire" movement recognizes the potential of sports to inspire courage, resilience, and unity and seeks to harness this power to counteract the pervasive influence of fear.

In this chapter, we meet Mia, a professional athlete and Olympic gold medallist who becomes an ambassador for the "Fear on Fire" movement. Mia understands the potential of sports to inspire people to overcome their fears, and she uses her platform to promote the values of courage, perseverance, and teamwork.

Mia works with sports organisations and community groups to create programs that encourage people of all ages and backgrounds to engage in sports and physical activities, emphasising the importance of overcoming personal fears and supporting one another. These programs not only improve participants' physical health but also foster a sense of unity and resilience, reflecting the core principles of the "Fear on Fire" movement.

As Mia's initiatives gain momentum, more athletes and sports organisations join the "Fear on Fire" movement, leading to a widespread effort to use sports as a tool to combat fear and promote unity. This transformation in the world of sports not only strengthens communities but also contributes to a more resilient, empathetic, and fearless society.

Mia's story demonstrates the power of sports in overcoming fear and showcases the potential for positive change when athletes and sports organisations embrace the principles of the "Fear on Fire" movement. As the movement continues to spread, more people within the sports industry are inspired to confront fear and work together to create a more courageous, united, and resilient world.

CHAPTER 58

FAITH AND SPIRITUALITY

A Source of Strength in a Fearful World

In a world where fear is pervasive, faith and spirituality can provide comfort, solace, and a sense of belonging to many individuals. The "Fear on Fire" movement recognizes the potential of faith and spirituality to inspire resilience and unite people, transcending cultural and religious differences.

In this chapter, we meet Aisha, a spiritual leader who becomes a prominent advocate for the "Fear on Fire" movement. Aisha is dedicated to using her faith as a source of strength and inspiration to help her community confront their fears and find inner peace.

Drawing on the core principles of the "Fear on Fire" movement, Aisha organises interfaith gatherings, where individuals from various religious and spiritual backgrounds come together to share their experiences, beliefs, and practices. These gatherings foster understanding, empathy, and unity, as participants find common ground in their shared desire to overcome fear and support one another.

Aisha's interfaith gatherings not only create a sense of belonging and unity among participants but also inspire them to take action in their own communities, spreading the principles of the "Fear on Fire" movement. As the movement gains momentum, more faith leaders and spiritual communities join the effort to promote resilience, understanding, and unity in the face of fear.

Aisha's story highlights the power of faith and spirituality in overcoming fear and showcases the potential for positive change when spiritual leaders and communities embrace the principles of the "Fear on Fire" movement. As the movement continues to spread, more people are inspired to draw on their faith and spirituality as a source of strength, fostering a more resilient, empathetic, and united world.

CHAPTER 59

THE TIPPING POINT

A World United Against Fear

As the "Fear on Fire" movement gains momentum, its impact becomes increasingly apparent. The chapters in this book have showcased the transformative power of fearlessness in various aspects of society, such as relationships, the workplace, politics, science and technology, media, entertainment, sports, faith, and mental health.

We witness the tipping point – a moment when the "Fear on Fire" movement reaches critical mass, sparking a global shift in attitude towards fear. As more individuals confront their fears and embrace the principles of the movement, they inspire others to do the same. The collective power of these fearless individuals leads to a more resilient, empathetic, and united world.

Key figures from various sectors, including politics, business, academia, and entertainment, come together to organise the first-ever Global Summit on Fearlessness. This event serves as a platform for leaders and experts to share their experiences, discuss strategies for overcoming fear, and forge partnerships to amplify the impact of the "Fear on Fire" movement.

The Global Summit on Fearlessness marks a turning point in human history, as people from all walks of life unite in their commitment to creating a more fearless and resilient world. This newfound sense of unity transcends borders, cultures, and ideologies, giving rise to a global community that is stronger, more compassionate, and better equipped to face the challenges of the future.

CHAPTER 60

THE ANATOMY OF FEAR

How Dictators Manipulate the Masses

In this section of the novel, we delve into the dark side of fear and its power to control and manipulate societies. Dictators throughout history have harnessed the power of fear to maintain their rule, suppress dissent, and prevent rebellion.

We introduce a fictional dictator, General Ivanov, who rules over a small, isolated country. General Ivanov's regime relies on fear to maintain control, using propaganda, censorship, and violence to keep the population in check.

The chapter explores the various strategies employed by General Ivanov and his regime to instil fear in the people.

The tactics include:

1. Propaganda: The regime uses state-controlled media to spread misinformation and create a narrative of external threats, painting General Ivanov as the only person capable of protecting the country from these dangers.

2. Censorship: The government strictly controls the flow of information, ensuring that dissenting voices are silenced, and only the official narrative reaches the people.

3. Surveillance: The regime employs a vast network of informants and state-of-the-art technology to monitor the population, creating an atmosphere of paranoia and distrust.

4. Violence and Repression: General Ivanov's regime brutally suppresses any signs of dissent or opposition, using torture, imprisonment, and public executions to send a clear message to the population: resistance is futile.

As the chapter unfolds, we begin to see the devastating impact of fear on the people living under General Ivanov's rule. The population is paralyzed by fear, unable to envision a better future or challenge the regime's authority. This chapter serves as a stark reminder of the destructive potential of fear when it is wielded as a weapon by those in power.

CHAPTER 61

SEEDS OF RESISTANCE

The Birth of a Rebellion

Despite General Ivanov's oppressive regime and the pervasive atmosphere of fear, a small group of courageous individuals decide to take a stand against tyranny. In Chapter 62, we meet the leaders of an underground resistance movement, including a former government official, a dissident journalist, and a fearless student activist.

The chapter explores how the resistance movement begins to take shape, with members using their unique skills and resources to challenge General Ivanov's rule. The group employs a variety of tactics, including:

1. Underground Networks: The resistance establishes a hidden network of safe houses and secret meeting places, allowing members to communicate, plan, and evade detection by the regime.

2. Propaganda of their Own: The dissident journalist uses her expertise to produce and distribute anti-regime leaflets and broadcasts, countering the government's narrative and inspiring hope in the oppressed population.

3. Acts of Defiance: The resistance carries out acts of nonviolent protest and sabotage, disrupting the regime's operations and demonstrating that General Ivanov's rule is not absolute.

4. Building Alliances: The resistance seeks out sympathetic individuals within the government and military, forging secret alliances that will be crucial to their eventual success.

As the resistance movement gains momentum, its members begin to realise the power of fearlessness in their fight against General Ivanov's regime. By confronting their own fears and standing up to the oppressive government, they inspire others to do the same, igniting a spark of hope in the hearts of the oppressed population.

CHAPTER 62

A FEARLESS ALLY

The Arrival of the "Fear on Fire" Movement

As the resistance movement continues to gain traction in their struggle against General Ivanov's regime, they receive an unexpected boost from an outside source: the "Fear on Fire" movement. Word of the global movement, which promotes fearlessness and resilience, reaches the oppressed country, inspiring hope and a renewed sense of determination in the hearts of the resistance members and the general population.

We follow the arrival of a "Fear on Fire" ambassador, Maya, who has made it her mission to support the resistance and spread the principles of the movement in the beleaguered nation. With her help, the resistance members learn to harness the power of fearlessness in their fight against tyranny.

Under Maya's guidance, the resistance employs the following strategies:

Empowerment through Fearlessness: Maya conducts workshops and training sessions to help resistance members confront and overcome their fears, equipping them with the mental and emotional strength needed to face the dangers and challenges ahead.

Building Bridges: Maya facilitates connections between the resistance and other "Fear on Fire" supporters around the world, creating a global network of allies who can provide resources, expertise, and moral support.

Expanding the Movement: Together with the resistance, Maya works to spread the message of fearlessness and resilience throughout the nation, reaching out to ordinary citizens who are tired of living in fear and yearning for change.

Amplifying Voices: The "Fear on Fire" movement helps to amplify the voices of the resistance, sharing their stories and struggles with the world and putting pressure on General Ivanov's regime.

CHAPTER 63

THE TURNING TIDE

Cracks in the Regime

As the "Fear on Fire" movement and the resistance continue their collaboration, their efforts begin to bear fruit. Chapter 64 sees the tide starting to turn against General Ivanov's regime, as fearlessness and resilience permeate the oppressed nation.

The chapter showcases the following developments:

Defections and Dissent: The regime's iron grip on its members begins to weaken, as some government officials, military personnel, and even members of General Ivanov's inner circle start to question their loyalty. Fear of the regime is replaced by fear of being on the wrong side of history.

Public Protests: Encouraged by the resistance and the "Fear on Fire" movement, more and more citizens take to the streets in peaceful demonstrations, demanding freedom, justice, and an end to General Ivanov's rule.

International Pressure: As the world witnesses the courageous acts of resistance and the suffering of the nation's people, international condemnation and pressure against General Ivanov's regime intensifies.

Diplomatic relations are strained, and economic sanctions are imposed, further weakening the dictator's hold on power.

The Power of Fearlessness: The once-paralyzed population now finds strength in their newfound fearlessness, as people from all walks of life stand together against tyranny. The sense of unity and determination that permeates the nation becomes a force that even General Ivanov cannot ignore.

CHAPTER 64

THE FALL OF GENERAL IVANOV

A Fearless Revolution

The relentless efforts of the resistance, the "Fear on Fire" movement, and the awakened population culminate in a decisive confrontation with General Ivanov's regime. As fearlessness sweeps through the nation, the once seemingly invincible dictator finds himself increasingly isolated and vulnerable.

The chapter chronicles the dramatic events that lead to the fall of General Ivanov, including:

1. A Defining Moment: A massive protest in the capital city serves as the catalyst for change, as millions of citizens gather to demand the end of General Ivanov's rule. The peaceful demonstration turns into a powerful display of unity and fearlessness that captures the attention of the world.

2. Defections and Resignations: Key members of the regime, including high-ranking military officers, abandon General Ivanov and join the resistance. With his power base crumbling, the dictator's authority is severely weakened.

3. The Final Stand: As the pressure mounts, General Ivanov orders a violent crackdown on the protests. However, the military and security forces, no longer blinded by fear, refuse to carry out the orders. The dictator's last-ditch effort to maintain control fails spectacularly.

4. The End of an Era: With the support of the international community, the resistance and the people of the nation seize the opportunity to topple General Ivanov's regime. The dictator is arrested, and the country embarks on a new chapter towards democracy and freedom.

CHAPTER 65

REBUILDING A NATION

Fearlessness and the Path to Democracy

With General Ivanov's regime toppled and the dictator behind bars, the nation faces the daunting task of rebuilding and healing after years of fear and oppression. Chapter 65 focuses on the efforts to establish a new democratic government, foster reconciliation, and address the wounds inflicted by the previous regime.

The chapter highlights the key steps taken to rebuild the nation and ensure a brighter future:

1. **Transitional Government:** The resistance, in collaboration with international partners, forms a transitional government that includes representatives from various factions, working together to establish a fair and democratic system.

2. **Constitutional Reforms:** The transitional government drafts a new constitution, enshrining the principles of democracy, human rights, and the rule of law. Citizens are invited to participate in the process, ensuring that their voices are heard.

3. **Truth and Reconciliation:** The nation embarks on a process of truth-telling and reconciliation, creating a platform for individuals to share their experiences of suffering and injustice during General Ivanov's rule. The process aims to promote healing and foster a sense of national unity.

4. **Empowerment through Education:** The new government prioritises education, focusing on instilling values of fearlessness, resilience, and critical thinking in future generations. This effort aims to prevent a return to dictatorship and nurture a population capable of safeguarding their newfound freedoms.

5. **International Support:** The international community, inspired by the nation's fearlessness and resilience, provides support through financial aid, expertise, and partnership. These resources help to bolster the nation's reconstruction and promote long-term stability.

CHAPTER 66

A FEARLESS LEGACY

Inspiring Global Change

As the once-oppressed nation continues its journey towards healing and democracy, the impact of the "Fear on Fire" movement and the resilience of the people in the face of tyranny capture the world's attention. The fearless revolution that toppled General Ivanov's regime serves as a source of inspiration and hope for others living under the shadow of fear and oppression.

In Chapter 66, we explore the ripple effects of the movement and the lasting impact it has on the global stage:

1. The Spread of the "Fear on Fire" Movement: The success of the movement in helping bring down a dictatorship encourages its expansion into other countries, where people are struggling to confront their fears and challenge oppressive systems.

2. **Grassroots Activism:** Activists and organisers from around the world, inspired by the fearless revolution, begin to apply the principles of fearlessness and resilience in their own

communities, sparking grassroots movements that tackle local and regional issues.

3. **International Policy and Diplomacy:** The events in the newly-liberated nation prompt a shift in international policies, as world leaders and organisations recognize the importance of addressing fear and promoting resilience as a means to foster peace, stability, and democracy.

4. **A New Era of Global Solidarity:** The story of the resistance and the "Fear on Fire" movement brings people from diverse backgrounds together, united in their pursuit of a world free from fear and oppression. This renewed sense of global solidarity leads to collaborative efforts to tackle shared challenges and promote a more just and equitable world.

CHAPTER 67

A NEW GENERATION OF FEARLESS LEADERS

As time passes, the once-oppressed nation begins to witness the emergence of a new generation of fearless leaders, nurtured by the values of the "Fear on Fire" movement and the lessons learned from the struggle against General Ivanov's regime. In Chapter 68, we explore the impact of these emerging leaders on the nation and the world.

This chapter highlights the following developments:

1. A Transformative Education: The nation's reformed education system, which emphasises the values of fearlessness, resilience, and critical thinking, empowers young people to become agents of positive change in their communities and beyond.

2. Diverse Representation: The new generation of leaders comes from a wide range of backgrounds, ensuring that diverse perspectives and experiences are represented in decision-making processes at all levels of society.

3. Tackling Global Challenges: These fearless leaders take on critical issues such as climate

change, poverty, and inequality, leveraging their resilience and fearlessness to drive innovative solutions and inspire collective action.

4. Strengthening Democracy: The new generation of leaders works tirelessly to consolidate and protect the democratic gains made since the fall of General Ivanov's regime, ensuring that the nation continues to move forward on the path of freedom, justice, and equality.

5. Inspiring Others: The example set by these young leaders resonates beyond the nation's borders, inspiring other young people around the world to confront their fears, challenge oppressive systems, and become agents of change in their own societies.

CHAPTER 68

JULIUS CAESAR AND THE TIDES OF POWER

In "Fear on Fire: Julius Caesar and the Fatal Power Struggle of the Roman Empire," we delve into the gripping tale of Julius Caesar's rise to power and the subsequent events that led to his tragic assassination. Caesar's increasing influence and dominance over Rome instilled fear in the hearts of the ruling elite, ultimately culminating in a plot to eliminate the perceived threat he posed to the established order.

The book takes readers on a journey through Caesar's early life, his military campaigns, and his political ambitions, which drove a wedge between him and the Roman Senate. As Caesar's power grew, so too did the fear and anxiety of the ruling class, who saw their traditional power base threatened by this charismatic and ambitious leader. This fear, fueled by the fire of Caesar's unrelenting ambition, created a volatile atmosphere that would ultimately lead to his demise.

The assassination of Julius Caesar serves as a powerful example of how fear can shape the course of history. The conspirators, driven by the fear of losing their power and status, took drastic measures to protect their interests, unwittingly setting the stage for the eventual downfalls of the Roman Republic and the rise of the Roman Empire. The story of Julius Caesar's life and death, as told in "Fear on Fire," is a cautionary tale about the dangers of unchecked ambition and the destructive power of fear in shaping the destinies of individuals and nations alike.

CHAPTER 69

A LASTING LEGACY

In the concluding chapter of the novel, we reflect on the lasting legacy of the "Fear on Fire" movement and its transformative impact on the once-oppressed nation and the world at large. The journey of the nation, from living under the shadow of fear and tyranny to becoming a beacon of hope, resilience, and fearlessness, serves as a powerful testament to the indomitable human spirit.

Key highlights of Chapter 69 include:

1. **A Nation Transformed:** The once-oppressed nation has risen from the ashes of dictatorship, establishing a thriving and inclusive democracy, a vibrant and diverse cultural landscape, and a new generation of fearless leaders.

2. **The Ripple Effect:** The principles and values of the "Fear on Fire" movement have inspired countless individuals and communities worldwide to confront their own fears, challenge oppressive systems, and build a more just and equitable world.

3. **The Power of Unity:** The story of the resistance and the "Fear on Fire" movement demonstrates that when people from diverse backgrounds and

experiences come together, united by a shared vision and purpose, they can overcome even the most formidable challenges.

4. **A Timeless Message:** The novel's message of fearlessness and resilience remains relevant and vital in a world that continues to grapple with fear and uncertainty. The story of the once-oppressed nation serves as a reminder that fear can be conquered and that resilience and hope can triumph in the face of adversity.

5. **An Ongoing Journey:** The story of the "Fear on Fire" movement and the once-oppressed nation does not end with the final chapter of the novel. Instead, it serves as an enduring source of inspiration and a call to action for readers to embrace fearlessness in their own lives, and to continue working towards a world that is free from fear and oppression.

CHAPTER 70

SPREADING THE FLAME

As the "Fear on Fire" movement continues to transform the lives of those within the once-oppressed nation, its message of hope and fearlessness begins to resonate far beyond its borders. This chapter follows the efforts of the movement's leaders and champions to spread the flame of fearlessness to other parts of the world, igniting change in the face of global challenges.

Key themes and developments in this chapter include:

1. International Recognition: The "Fear on Fire" movement garners worldwide attention for its remarkable achievements, prompting other nations to take notice and consider adopting similar principles to combat fear and oppression in their own societies.

2. Global Advocacy: Fearless leaders from the once-oppressed nation embark on a mission to share their experiences and insights, advocating for human rights, social justice, and the power of fearlessness in confronting global issues.

3. Cross-Cultural Collaboration: The "Fear on Fire" movement inspires new partnerships and collaborations between individuals and

organisations from different cultural backgrounds, fostering a global network of fearless change-makers.

4. The Fearless Ambassadors: A group of dedicated individuals from the once-oppressed nation, known as the Fearless Ambassadors, travel to different countries to share their stories and provide support to those facing fear and oppression. Their efforts help ignite the fire of fearlessness in countless hearts across the globe.

5. A Global Movement: As the flame of fearlessness spreads, the "Fear on Fire" movement evolves into a global force for change, with people from diverse backgrounds and experiences uniting under its banner to tackle fear and injustice.

CHAPTER 71

THE FEARLESS SUMMIT

As the "Fear on Fire" movement continues to grow and expand, a significant event takes place, further solidifying its impact on a global scale. This chapter centres around the organisation of the first-ever Fearless Summit, a gathering of fearless leaders, activists, and change-makers from around the world, aiming to share knowledge, resources, and strategies in the fight against fear and oppression.

Key themes and developments in this chapter include:

1. A United Vision: Representatives from diverse nations and backgrounds come together at the Fearless Summit, united by their shared commitment to overcoming fear and fostering a more just and equitable world.

2. Sharing Experiences: Participants at the summit share their personal stories of fear, resilience, and triumph, inspiring others with their experiences and fostering a greater sense of empathy and understanding among the attendees.

3. Collaborative Strategies: Workshops and panel discussions at the Fearless Summit focus on developing collaborative strategies to address the

root causes of fear and oppression, highlighting the importance of working together across borders and cultures to create lasting change.

4. Global Initiatives: The summit serves as the launching point for several global initiatives aimed at combating fear and promoting fearlessness, including educational programs, mentorship opportunities, and grassroots activism.

5. A Lasting Impact: The Fearless Summit not only strengthens the bonds between fearless leaders and change-makers but also inspires countless others worldwide to join the "Fear on Fire" movement and take action in their own communities.

CHAPTER 72

THE POWER OF ONE

While the Fearless Summit's global impact is undeniable, this chapter brings the focus back to the individual level, highlighting the extraordinary power and influence one person can have in the fight against fear and oppression. Through a series of personal vignettes, this chapter demonstrates the ways in which ordinary people can inspire change within their own communities and beyond.

Key themes and developments in this chapter include:

1. Overcoming Personal Fear: A young activist from a small village shares her journey of overcoming fear to stand up against a corrupt local government, inspiring others in her community to join her cause.

2. Breaking Barriers: A prominent business leader from a minority community defies societal expectations and fear of failure to become a trailblazer in her industry, paving the way for future generations to follow in her footsteps.

3. Fostering Dialogue: A teacher in a conflict-ridden region uses the principles of the "Fear on Fire" movement to create a safe space for students

from opposing sides to engage in open dialogue, promoting understanding and empathy among the next generation.

4. Spreading the Flame: An artist harnesses the power of creative expression to raise awareness of the "Fear on Fire" movement, using her work to inspire others to confront their fears and become agents of change in their own lives.

5. A Ripple Effect: As each individual shares their story and embraces fearlessness, they inspire others to do the same, creating a ripple effect of change that extends far beyond their immediate circles.

In this Chapter, the "Fear on Fire" movement is shown to be not just a global phenomenon but also a deeply personal journey for each individual involved. By focusing on the power of one, this chapter serves as a reminder that every person has the potential to make a difference in the fight against fear and oppression.

CHAPTER 73

UNITED IN FEARLESSNESS

The "Fear on Fire" movement experiences a critical turning point as people from different countries, cultures, and walks of life come together in a display of unity and fearlessness. This chapter explores the significance of this moment and the impact it has on the global fight against fear and oppression.

Key themes and developments in this chapter include

1. A Worldwide Protest: A massive, coordinated demonstration takes place across the globe, with millions of people taking to the streets to stand against fear and demand a more just and equitable world.

2. Cross-Cultural Solidarity: As the worldwide protest unfolds, people from different cultural backgrounds join forces, setting aside their differences to unite under the banner of fearlessness and demonstrate their commitment to a shared cause.

3. The Power of Social Media: The global protest gains momentum and visibility through the power of social media, as participants share images and stories of fearlessness, inspiring

others to join the movement and make their voices heard.

4. Fearless Leaders Emerge: Throughout the worldwide protest, new leaders emerge from various communities, taking up the mantle of fearlessness and guiding others in their pursuit of a more just and equitable future.

5. A Pivotal Moment: The global protest serves as a pivotal moment in the "Fear on Fire" movement, marking a shift in public opinion and galvanising support for the cause. As a result, governments and institutions around the world begin to take notice and evaluate their policies and practices related to fear and oppression.

CHAPTER 74

THE NEXT GENERATION

The focus shifts to the next generation, who are poised to carry the torch of the "Fear on Fire" movement into the future. This chapter explores the ways in which young people are embracing fearlessness and using it as a tool for change within their own lives and communities.

Key themes and developments in this chapter include:

1. Youth Empowerment: With the support of fearless mentors and role models, young people are encouraged to confront their fears, develop their leadership skills, and take an active role in shaping their communities and the world.

2. Education for Fearlessness: Schools and educational institutions around the world begin to integrate principles of fearlessness into their curricula, fostering a generation of critical thinkers and change-makers who are unafraid to challenge the status quo.

3. Harnessing Creativity: Young artists, musicians, and writers use their talents to express and promote the message of the "Fear on Fire"

movement, inspiring their peers and older generations alike with their fearless creativity.

4. Technological Innovations: The next generation leverages advances in technology to amplify the impact of the "Fear on Fire" movement, using social media, virtual reality, and other innovative tools to connect with like-minded individuals around the world and raise awareness of the fight against fear and oppression.

5. A Legacy of Fearlessness: As the next generation takes up the mantle of the "Fear on Fire" movement, they ensure that the message of fearlessness is passed down to future generations, creating a lasting legacy of courage, resilience, and hope.

CHAPTER 75

BUILDING A FEARLESS WORLD

The practical steps and strategies that individuals, communities, and nations can adopt to build a more fearless world. This chapter provides a roadmap for implementing the principles of the "Fear on Fire" movement on a global scale and offers guidance on overcoming the challenges that may arise along the way.

Key themes and developments in this chapter include:

1. Fostering Dialogue: Encouraging open and honest conversations among people with diverse perspectives is crucial for building understanding and empathy, ultimately leading to the dismantling of fear and prejudice.

2. Prioritising Mental Health: Recognizing the role of fear in mental health issues and providing accessible resources and support can help individuals overcome their fears and lead more fulfilling lives.

3. Promoting Equality and Social Justice: Addressing systemic inequalities and injustices that perpetuate fear and division is essential for creating a more just and fearless world.

4. Encouraging Global Collaboration: Fostering international partnerships and cooperation can help nations work together to tackle shared fears, such as climate change, terrorism, and poverty.

5. Celebrating Fearlessness: By sharing stories of fearlessness and recognizing the achievements of those who have stood up against fear and oppression, society can cultivate a culture of courage and resilience.

CHAPTER 76

FEAR ON FIRE – THE LEGACY

The story of the "Fear on Fire" movement reaches its climax, as the collective efforts of individuals, communities, and nations begin to create lasting change. This chapter reflects on the progress made and the lessons learned throughout the journey, while also looking ahead to the challenges and opportunities that lie ahead.

Key themes and developments in this chapter include

1. Recognizing Progress: As the world continues to embrace fearlessness, progress is made in various areas, including social justice, mental health, and international relations. The successes achieved along the way serve as a testament to the power of collective action and perseverance.

2. Learning from the Past: The story of the "Fear on Fire" movement highlights the importance of learning from history and using past experiences as a guide for moving forward. Acknowledging past mistakes and working to prevent their repetition is crucial for building a more fearless future.

3. Adapting to New Challenges: As the world evolves, new challenges and fears will inevitably arise. The "Fear on Fire" movement must remain adaptive and resilient, continually updating its strategies and approaches to meet these emerging challenges head-on.

4. Empowering Future Generations: Ensuring that the legacy of fearlessness endures requires a continued focus on youth empowerment and education. By nurturing the potential of future generations, the "Fear on Fire" movement can help to create a world where fear no longer holds sway over the human experience.

5. A Lasting Impact: The "Fear on Fire" movement has the potential to leave a lasting impact on the world, changing the course of history and transforming the lives of millions for the better. As the movement continues to grow and evolve, its influence will reverberate across the globe for generations to come.

CHAPTER 77

SUSTAINING THE FLAME

The focus shifts to the importance of sustaining the momentum of the "Fear on Fire" movement in the face of an ever-changing world. This chapter examines the strategies and approaches necessary to ensure that the principles of fearlessness remain ingrained in society and continue to inspire positive change.

Key themes and developments in this chapter include:

1. Building Resilient Communities: Encouraging individuals and communities to work together, share resources, and support one another is vital for fostering resilience in the face of fear and adversity.

2. Strengthening Global Networks: Maintaining strong connections and collaboration among nations and organisations dedicated to the "Fear on Fire" movement helps to amplify its impact and ensure that its message reaches a wider audience.

3. Investing in Education and Awareness: Providing ongoing education and raising awareness about the consequences of fear and the benefits of fearlessness is crucial for keeping the principles

of the "Fear on Fire" movement alive and relevant.

4. Inspiring Future Leaders: Identifying and nurturing emerging leaders who embody the values of fearlessness and are committed to carrying the "Fear on Fire" moving forward is essential for ensuring its long-term success.

5. Adapting to Evolving Challenges: Recognizing that the nature of fear will continue to evolve, the "Fear on Fire" movement must remain flexible and responsive to new threats and challenges, developing innovative solutions to confront fear in all its forms.

CHAPTER 78

THE RIPPLE EFFECT OF COURAGE

The story delves into the broader consequences of the "Fear on Fire" movement, illustrating how courage and fearlessness can create a ripple effect that touches every aspect of society. This chapter explores the impact of a world where fear no longer dominates, and the potential for a brighter future emerges.

Key themes and developments in this chapter include:

1. A Shift in Social Dynamics: As fear recedes, communities become more cohesive and supportive, with people working together to overcome challenges and create a better world for all.

2. The Power of Individual Courage: The stories of everyday heroes who have embraced fearlessness serve as an inspiration to others, proving that one person's courageous actions can have a profound impact on the lives of many.

3. Economic Growth and Prosperity: Freed from the constraints of fear, individuals and businesses can thrive, leading to greater innovation, economic growth, and prosperity on a global scale.

4. Conflict Resolution and Peace: As nations embrace fearlessness, the focus shifts from competition and conflict to cooperation and understanding, fostering peace and diplomatic solutions to global issues.

5. Environmental Progress: With fear no longer holding back efforts to address climate change and protect the planet, significant progress is made towards a more sustainable and environmentally conscious world.

CHAPTER 79

THE AWAKENING OF FEARLESS HEROES

The narrative delves into the personal journeys of several individuals from different walks of life, whose fear has been ignited by the "Fear on Fire" movement, driving them to make transformative changes in their lives and the world around them. This chapter highlights the power of fearlessness and the impact it can have on individuals, communities, and society as a whole.

1. The Reluctant Leader: Maria, a shy and introverted woman, finds herself thrust into a leadership role in her community after a natural disaster. Initially overwhelmed by her fears, she discovers the courage to take charge and guide her community through the crisis. Maria's newfound fearlessness inspires others to join her in rebuilding their town, leading to a stronger and more united community.

2. The Fearful Entrepreneur: Raj, a talented but risk-averse entrepreneur, struggles to take the plunge and start his own business. Inspired by the "Fear on Fire" movement, he confronts his fears and launches a social enterprise that

empowers disadvantaged individuals. Raj's business thrives, creating jobs and making a significant impact on the lives of those it serves.

3. The Anxious Activist: Mei, a young woman plagued by anxiety, finds her voice and passion for environmental activism after attending a "Fear on Fire" event. Determined to overcome her fears, Mei becomes a driving force in her community's efforts to combat climate change. Her tireless work and dedication inspire others to join the fight for a sustainable future.

4. The Former Follower: Jamal, a disillusioned former member of a violent extremist group, seeks redemption after witnessing the devastating effects of fear on his community. Embracing the principles of the "Fear on Fire" movement, Jamal turns his life around and dedicates himself to promoting peace and understanding among people of different faiths and backgrounds.

5. The Burnt-Out Executive: Ellen, a high-powered executive, is brought to the brink of burnout by the constant fear of failure and the relentless pressure to succeed. After discovering the "Fear on Fire" movement, Ellen decides to leave her corporate job and dedicate her life to helping others overcome their fears. As a coach and

motivational speaker, she empowers countless individuals to live more fulfilling and fearless lives.

The journeys of these five individuals intertwine, creating a powerful tapestry of courage and transformation. As their stories unfold, it becomes evident that the "Fear on Fire" movement has the potential to ignite the flame of fearlessness in anyone, regardless of their background or circumstances. Each character serves as a testament to the power of embracing fear and using it as a catalyst for positive change, both personally and on a broader scale. As the chapter concludes, the impact of their actions ripples outwards, inspiring others to confront their own fears and contribute to a more courageous and compassionate world.

CHAPTER 80

UNLIKELY ALLIANCES

The narrative highlights the importance of collaboration and unity in the face of fear. The five characters introduced in Chapter 81, with their diverse backgrounds and unique experiences, come together to form an unlikely alliance. By joining forces, they amplify the impact of the "Fear on Fire" movement and demonstrate the power of cooperation.

1. Connecting the Dots: As the characters interact and share their stories, they discover commonalities and recognize the strength in their diversity. Maria's leadership skills, Raj's entrepreneurial spirit, Mei's passion for the environment, Jamal's commitment to peace, and Ellen's ability to inspire are all essential pieces of the puzzle, creating a powerful synergy.

2. A Shared Vision: Despite their differences, the characters find common ground in their desire to build a more fearless and just society. They realise that together, they can create a more significant impact than they ever could have achieved individually.

3. Building Bridges: As the group collaborates on various projects and initiatives, they work to bridge the gaps between different communities, industries, and social issues. Their efforts foster understanding, break down barriers, and create new opportunities for people from all walks of life to confront their fears and embrace fearlessness.

4. Expanding the Movement: Leveraging their unique skills, experiences, and networks, the characters work to spread the "Fear on Fire" message far and wide. They organise workshops, seminars, and events, reaching out to people across the globe and inspiring countless individuals to join the movement and confront their fears.

5. The Ripple Effect Continues: As the characters' stories become more widely known, their impact continues to grow. They inspire others to form their own unlikely alliances, bringing together people from different backgrounds and uniting them under the banner of fearlessness.

CHAPTER 81

EMBRACING VULNERABILITY

The narrative delves deeper into the characters' personal struggles, showcasing their vulnerability as they navigate the challenges of embracing fearlessness. As the five heroes confront their own fears and insecurities, they learn valuable lessons about the power of vulnerability and the importance of being true to themselves.

1. Maria's Struggle: Though Maria has become a strong leader for her community, she wrestles with the fear of being exposed as a fraud. She learns to accept her imperfections and embrace her vulnerability, realising that her honesty and authenticity make her a more effective and relatable leader.

2. Raj's Reluctance: Raj finds it difficult to trust others with the responsibility of managing his social enterprise, fearing that they might fail. He learns to let go of control and allow others to take on leadership roles, discovering the importance of vulnerability in fostering collaboration and teamwork.

3. Mei's Anxiety: Despite her passion for environmental activism, Mei still struggles with anxiety and self-doubt. As she learns to embrace her vulnerability and share her struggles with others, she finds support and understanding within her community, helping her to become a more resilient and courageous activist.

4. Jamal's Guilt: Jamal grapples with the guilt and shame of his past involvement in a violent extremist group. By opening up about his experiences and embracing vulnerability, he is able to heal and move forward, using his story as a powerful testimony to the transformative power of fearlessness and redemption.

5. Ellen's Quest for Balance: In her pursuit of helping others overcome their fears, Ellen finds herself neglecting her own well-being. She learns the importance of self-care and embracing vulnerability, understanding that she can only help others if she is willing to take care of herself first.

CHAPTER 82

THE POWER OF COMMUNITY

The narrative emphasises the crucial role that the community plays in overcoming fear and fostering fearlessness. As the five characters continue to collaborate and grow, they come to understand the importance of connecting with others and building a supportive network.

1. A Network of Support: The characters realise that their individual efforts can only go so far in fighting fear. They begin to reach out to others, sharing their stories and experiences, and in the process, they create a network of individuals who are dedicated to embracing fearlessness.

2. Collaborative Initiatives: As the "Fear on Fire" movement grows, the characters work together on various projects to help spread their message of courage and resilience. They organise community events, support groups, and educational programs, harnessing the collective strength of their network.

3. Strength in Numbers: The characters find that their community's support gives them the strength to face their fears and challenges. They

learn that they are not alone in their struggles and that by leaning on one another, they can achieve far more than they ever could have imagined.

4. Inspiring Change: The power of community begins to inspire change on a broader scale. As more people join the "Fear on Fire" movement and share their stories, they create a ripple effect that extends far beyond their immediate network, sparking a global shift towards fearlessness.

5. A Lasting Legacy: The characters come to understand that their impact is not only defined by their individual achievements but also by the community they have built. By fostering a strong and supportive network, they ensure that their message of fearlessness continues to inspire and empower future generations.

CHAPTER 83

UNEXPECTED CHALLENGES

The "Fear on Fire" movement faces unexpected challenges that test the resilience and determination of the characters and their community. As they confront these obstacles, the characters learn valuable lessons about adaptability, perseverance, and the importance of remaining united in the face of adversity.

1. A Sudden Loss: Tragedy strikes when one of the founding members of the "Fear on Fire" movement passes away unexpectedly. The characters and their community are devastated, but they rally together, finding strength in their shared grief and honouring their fallen comrade's memory by continuing their work.

2. Resistance from Authorities: As the movement gains traction, it attracts the attention of government officials who view it as a potential threat. The characters must navigate a delicate balance between standing up for their beliefs and avoiding unnecessary confrontation, learning the importance of strategic thinking and diplomacy.

3. Miscommunication and Conflict: As the community grows, misunderstandings and

differences in opinion arise, leading to conflicts within the group. The characters learn to navigate these challenges by fostering open communication, active listening, and empathy, strengthening the bonds within their community.

4. Financial Struggles: The "Fear on Fire" movement faces financial difficulties as they struggle to secure funding for their initiatives. The characters must think creatively and collaborate to find new sources of support, learning the value of resourcefulness and determination in overcoming challenges.

5. Unwavering Commitment: Despite the setbacks they face, the characters and their community remain unwavering in their commitment to the "Fear on Fire" movement. They learn that adversity can be a powerful catalyst for growth and change and that by standing together, they can weather any storm.

CHAPTER 84

THE POWER OF FORGIVENESS

The characters learn the importance of forgiveness in overcoming fear and fostering personal growth. As they face their past mistakes and seek to make amends, they discover that the journey towards fearlessness is also one of healing and self-discovery.

1. Maria's Reconciliation: Maria confronts the strained relationship with her estranged father, learning to let go of past hurts and embracing the power of forgiveness. As she heals, she finds a newfound sense of inner strength and self-worth.

2. Raj's Redemption: Raj struggles with guilt over past business decisions that negatively impacted others. He sets out on a path of making amends and, through forgiveness, learns to accept his past while forging a new, ethical path forward.

3. Mei's Self-Forgiveness: Mei grapples with feelings of inadequacy and failure as she faces setbacks in her activism. By learning to forgive herself and embrace her imperfections, she discovers that her resilience and determination are her greatest strengths.

4. Jamal's Transformation: Jamal seeks forgiveness from those he hurt during his time with the extremist group. In the process, he not only finds redemption but also inspires others with his story of change and the healing power of forgiveness.

5. Ellen's Compassion: Ellen learns to forgive herself for neglecting her own well-being in her pursuit of helping others. As she practises self-compassion, she becomes a more effective and empathetic leader, inspiring others to embrace self-forgiveness and healing.

CHAPTER 85

THE TURNING POINT

The "Fear on Fire" movement faces a pivotal moment that will determine its future. The characters must confront their own fears and doubts as they navigate this turning point, ultimately deciding the path they will take moving forward.

1. Maria's Choice: Maria faces a difficult decision between pursuing her newfound passion for helping others heal and accepting a prestigious job offer that would secure her financial future. By confronting her fears and embracing her true calling, Maria solidifies her commitment to the movement.

2. Raj's Sacrifice: Raj's company is offered a lucrative deal that would require him to compromise his ethical values. After wrestling with his fears of financial insecurity, Raj ultimately decides to stand firm in his principles, further cementing his dedication to the "Fear on Fire" movement.

3. Mei's Stand: Mei's activism is challenged by a powerful opposition, forcing her to decide between backing down or risking personal

consequences. Her courageous decision to stand her ground inspires others and solidifies her role as a leader in the movement.

4. Jamal's Test: Jamal is offered a chance to rejoin his former extremist group in exchange for protection from those who still seek revenge for his past actions. Despite his fears, Jamal remains committed to his new path, demonstrating his unwavering dedication to the "Fear on Fire" movement.

5. Ellen's Leadership: As the movement faces internal divisions and external pressures, Ellen must confront her own fears and doubts about her ability to lead. By embracing her strengths and learning from her weaknesses, Ellen solidifies her role as a guiding force for the movement.

CHAPTER 86

GANDHI'S NON-VIOLENCE MOVEMENT AND INDIA'S PATH TO FREEDOM"

In "Fear on Fire: Gandhi's Non-Violence Movement and the Path to India's Freedom," the reader is taken on a historical journey through the Indian independence movement led by Mahatma Gandhi. This inspiring story demonstrates how the power of non-violence and the ability to confront fear can create a lasting change.

Through the perspective of the British Raj, the fear of losing control over India became increasingly apparent, as Gandhi's non-violent approach gained momentum and garnered international attention. The fear of growing resistance and the potential for escalating violence ultimately led the British to reconsider their position and grant India its independence.

This book explores how Gandhi and his followers harnessed the power of 'Fear on Fire,' turning the British government's fear into a catalyst for change. By embracing their own fears and channelling them towards a peaceful yet resolute resistance, the Indian people were able to achieve freedom from British rule.

The lessons from Gandhi's non-violent movement resonate today, reminding us that fear can be transformed into a driving force for positive change when confronted head-on and with unwavering determination.

CHAPTER 87

SHAKESPEARE AND THE TRIUMPH OVER FEAR

William Shakespeare, known as one of the greatest playwrights and poets in history, also grappled with fear throughout his life and work. His understanding of human nature and the complexities of the human experience allowed him to create timeless characters and stories that continue to resonate with audiences today.

In his plays, Shakespeare often explored themes of fear, anxiety, and insecurity. For instance, in "Macbeth," the title character's fear of losing power drives him to commit heinous acts, ultimately leading to his downfall. Similarly, in "Hamlet," the protagonist's fear of making the wrong decision and the uncertainty of what lies beyond death lead to his inaction and, eventually, tragedy.

Shakespeare himself may have experienced fears and anxieties as an artist in his own right. The competitive world of the Elizabethan theatre was unforgiving, and the pressure to create successful plays could have been immense. Additionally, the fear of censorship or persecution during a time of religious and political upheaval may have weighed heavily on his mind.

However, instead of succumbing to these fears, Shakespeare channelled them into his work, transforming them into powerful and thought-provoking themes that continue to captivate readers and audiences. By exploring and examining fear in his characters and stories, he was able to gain a deeper understanding of the human experience and create timeless works that have cemented his place in history as one of the world's most prominent literary figures.

CHAPTER 88

CHRISTIANITY'S JOURNEY THROUGH HISTORY

Christianity's emergence as one of the world's major religions can be connected to various instances of "Fear on Fire." Jesus Christ, the central figure of Christianity, did not explicitly mention or establish the religion during his lifetime. However, his teachings and actions sparked the development of the Christian faith.

After Jesus' crucifixion and resurrection, his followers faced significant fear and persecution. The early Christian community faced the fear of violence, social ostracism, and even death for their beliefs. In the face of these challenges, the "Fear on Fire" concept can be seen in the unwavering commitment and resolve of Jesus' disciples to spread his message of love, compassion, and salvation. They transformed their fear into a driving force that propelled the growth of Christianity.

The Roman Empire initially persecuted Christians, but this persecution only served to strengthen the resolve of the early Christian community. This can be seen as another example of "Fear on Fire," where fear led to increased dedication to the faith. The fear of persecution ultimately resulted in the expansion of Christianity, as people were inspired by the resilience and convictions of the early followers of Jesus.

In 313 CE, the Edict of Milan, issued by Roman Emperor Constantine, granted religious tolerance to Christianity, which led to its rapid growth and eventual establishment as the official religion of the Roman Empire in 380 CE. This development is another manifestation of "Fear on Fire," as the fear of persecution gave way to the widespread adoption and growth of the Christian faith.

In conclusion, the development and spread of Christianity can be connected to the concept of "Fear on Fire," where fear was transformed into a catalyst for change and growth. The early followers of Jesus overcame their fears, which ultimately led to the establishment of one of the world's largest religions.

CHAPTER 89

FINLAND JOINS NATO AMID GROWING GLOBAL TENSIONS

In this chapter, we delve into the geopolitical circumstances that led to Finland's decision to join the North Atlantic Treaty Organization (NATO) in April 2023, following Russia's invasion of Ukraine. This case demonstrates how 'fear on fire' can impact international relations and prompt nations to seek security through alliances.

Finland, a nation historically known for its policy of neutrality, began reconsidering its position in the face of escalating global tensions. Following Russia's annexation of Crimea in 2014, Finland observed a shift in the European security landscape and experienced increased military activities in its vicinity. This development sparked a national debate over the necessity of joining NATO to ensure the country's long-term security.

The Russian invasion of Ukraine in 2022 served as a catalyst for Finland's decision to seek NATO membership. This act of aggression heightened concerns over the stability of the region and the potential threat posed to Finland's sovereignty. In response, Finnish leaders initiated the process of joining the alliance, engaging in extensive diplomatic negotiations and fulfilling the required military and political commitments.

Finally, on 4th April 2023, Finland was welcomed as the latest member of NATO. This decision was driven by 'fear on fire', as Finland sought to safeguard its security and strengthen its position in an increasingly unpredictable global environment. By joining NATO, Finland aimed to deter potential threats and contribute to the collective defence of its fellow member states.

Through this example, the chapter emphasises the role of fear in shaping national security policies and alliances, showcasing how 'Fear on Fire' can be harnessed to drive strategic decisions and adapt to a rapidly evolving geopolitical landscape.

CHAPTER 90

THE PYRAMIDS OF EGYPT AND THE GREAT WALL OF CHINA

In this chapter, we explore the historical motivations behind two of the most monumental constructions in human history: the Pyramids of Egypt and the Great Wall of China. These awe-inspiring feats of engineering are not only symbols of their respective civilizations but also powerful examples of how 'Fear on Fire' has driven humanity to create extraordinary structures.

The construction of the Egyptian pyramids was fueled by the pharaohs' fear of their own mortality and their desire to preserve their legacy for eternity. These colossal tombs were designed to protect the pharaoh's body and ensure a successful journey to the afterlife. The immense resources and labour required for their construction demonstrate the power of fear in driving such a monumental undertaking.

Similarly, the Great Wall of China was driven by 'fear on fire' The Chinese emperors were fearful of invasions from the nomadic tribes of the north and sought to protect their kingdom by constructing a massive defensive barrier. Spanning thousands of miles and taking centuries to complete, the Great Wall stands as a testament to the determination of the Chinese people and the lengths they were willing to go to protect their civilization from external threats.

These historical examples highlight the power of fear on fire in shaping human history and inspiring grand architectural achievements. By understanding the motivations behind such constructions, readers can gain insight into the ways in which fear has driven people to create lasting legacies and protect their civilizations. Furthermore, these stories serve as a reminder of the potential for greatness that can emerge when humanity confronts its fears and channels them into transformative endeavours.

CHAPTER 91

FROM FEAR TO UNITY

The Impact of World Wars and the Formation of the United Nations

In this chapter, we delve into the events surrounding the World Wars and how fear fueled the devastating conflicts that ultimately led to the formation of the United Nations and the emergence of a new world order. The fear of domination and loss of sovereignty, combined with escalating tensions between nations, ignited the flames of World War I and World War II, resulting in the death and suffering of millions.

The aftermath of these wars brought about a profound realisation of the need for international cooperation and unity. 'Fear on fire' had left the world in ruins, and it was clear that a new approach was necessary to prevent such catastrophes from recurring. This realisation gave birth to the United Nations, an organisation dedicated to promoting peace, security, and international cooperation.

The UN has played a critical role in addressing global challenges and fostering diplomacy, demonstrating the power of unity in overcoming fear. The new world order, led by the United States and its allies, has sought to maintain peace and stability through international institutions, economic cooperation, and collective security.

As we reflect on the lessons of the World Wars and the formation of the United Nations, the importance of overcoming the "Fear on Fire" and embracing unity, diplomacy, and cooperation becomes clear. By working together, nations can build a more peaceful and prosperous world for future generations.

CHAPTER 92

A SPIRITUAL JOURNEY

Siddhartha's Path to Enlightenment

In this chapter, we explore the story of Siddhartha Gautama, who would later become the Buddha. Born into a life of luxury and shielded from the harsh realities of the world, Siddhartha's father was driven by fear, as he attempted to prevent his son from encountering the suffering predicted by astrologers and spiritual gurus. However, fate had other plans, and Siddhartha's curiosity about the world beyond the palace walls led him to witness the Four Sights, which would forever change his life.

These Four Sights – an old man, a sick man, a corpse, and a holy man – served as a catalyst for Siddhartha's spiritual journey. They exposed him to the truth of human suffering and set him on a path of self-discovery, seeking to find a way to end suffering for all. Through meditation and deep introspection, Siddhartha eventually attained enlightenment and became the Buddha, sharing his insights with the world.

The story of Siddhartha serves as a powerful example of how fear can shape our lives and decisions, but also how overcoming that fear can lead to personal growth and transformation. By confronting the realities of the world and embracing a spiritual path, Siddhartha was able to transcend his father's fear and become a guiding light for humanity.

CHAPTER 93

IGNITING CHANGE: BOLLYWOOD

In the wake of the COVID-19 pandemic, the Indian Bollywood industry faced a crisis like never before, with millions of workers affected and the box office hitting rock bottom. More than 30 movies were released, but none of them managed to break even, including films featuring top superstars like Salman Khan, Aamir Khan, Shah Rukh Khan, Ajay Devgan, and Akshay Kumar.

As panic set in, many industry players shifted their focus to TV screenings, Amazon Prime Video, Netflix, and other OTT platforms. Some superstars began investing in South Indian movies. However, Shah Rukh Khan recognized the widespread fear and decided to adopt a "Fear on Fire" strategy to revive the industry.

Abandoning traditional marketing approaches, Shah Rukh Khan devised a new movie marketing strategy specifically for his film "Pathaan." This innovative approach turned the tide and led to astounding success, with the film grossing $130 million (1023 crores) in just four months, breaking all previous Bollywood records. This remarkable turnaround exemplified the power of the "Fear on Fire" approach to confront adversity, ignite change, and achieve extraordinary results

CHAPTER 94

EMBRACING VULNERABILITY

The focus shifts to the importance of embracing vulnerability in the "Fear on Fire" movement, showcasing how acknowledging and sharing one's fears and insecurities can lead to deeper connections, personal growth, and societal change.

1. The Power of Vulnerability: The story delves into the concept of vulnerability as a strength, highlighting how admitting and sharing one's fears can lead to personal growth, authentic connections, and increased empathy.

2. Support Networks: As more individuals embrace vulnerability and share their fears, support networks of friends, families, and communities grow stronger and more resilient, providing a safe space for personal growth and healing.

3. Redefining Success: Society begins to redefine success, moving away from material wealth and status, and instead prioritising emotional well-being, personal growth, and the ability to confront and overcome fear.

4. The Role of Art and Creativity: The chapter explores the role of art and creativity in

expressing vulnerability and confronting fear, showcasing how various art forms can serve as powerful tools for healing, self-discovery, and social change.

5. A Global Movement: Embracing vulnerability becomes a key aspect of the "Fear on Fire" movement, inspiring individuals from all corners of the world to face their fears, share their stories, and create a more compassionate and connected global community.

CHAPTER 95

MOMENTS OF FEAR ON FIRE

The story delves into the moments where individuals from various walks of life experience their "Fear on Fire," highlighting the transformative power of confronting and overcoming fear in even the most challenging circumstances.

1. The Soldier in Battle: Amidst the chaos and uncertainty of war, a soldier draws upon their inner strength and courage to face their fears, ultimately making life-saving decisions and forming deep bonds with their comrades.

2. The Prisoner on Death Row: On their final day, a prisoner confronts their fear of death and their past mistakes, leading to a profound moment of self-reflection, acceptance, and inner peace.

3. The Hospital Patient Before Brain Surgery: As a patient faces the daunting prospect of brain surgery, they grapple with their fears and uncertainties, ultimately finding solace in the love and support of their family and the skilled medical team.

4. The Astronaut on a Planet Landing: As an astronaut embarks on a ground-breaking mission

to land on a new planet, they confront their fears of the unknown and embrace the potential for discovery and scientific advancement.

5. The Child on Their First Day of School: A young child navigates the anxiety and excitement of their first day of school, facing their fears and learning to adapt to a new environment, forging friendships, and building self-confidence.

CHAPTER 96

BREAKING THE DOLLAR'S DOMINANCE

For nearly seven decades, the US dollar has reigned supreme as the world's dominant currency, serving as the reserve currency for almost 98% of countries. This status has given the United States immense financial power and influence over global markets. However, recent geopolitical tensions and economic rivalries have incited fear among many developing nations, who have started to question their reliance on the US dollar.

The growing competition between the US and China, coupled with a long-term cold war with Russia, has exacerbated these fears. Additionally, the US has employed punitive measures against rogue states, such as freezing their financial assets, further unnerving countries that worry about the potential consequences of US dollar dominance.

These concerns led to the formation of BRICS, an alliance comprising Brazil, Russia, India, China, and South Africa. BRICS aims to reduce its member countries' dependence on the US dollar and establish a common currency for trade. This bold move is an attempt to mitigate the risks associated with the existing financial system and create a more balanced global economy.

The development of the New Development Bank (NDB) by BRICS is another step towards a more diversified financial system. The NDB's purpose is to finance infrastructure and sustainable development projects in BRICS countries and other developing economies, further reducing reliance on traditional Western-backed financial institutions like the World Bank and the International Monetary Fund.

Moreover, BRICS countries have initiated bilateral and multilateral currency swap agreements, allowing them to trade using their local currencies instead of the US dollar. These agreements enhance economic cooperation and stability among member nations, strengthening their collective financial resilience.

This shift away from US dollar dominance serves as another example of the 'Fear on Fire' phenomenon, as nations band together to build an alternative financial system for the future. This movement, fueled by fear and ambition, has the potential to reshape the global economic landscape, challenging the established order and paving the way for new possibilities.

CHAPTER 97

THE CLIMATE CRISES

The world was facing a crisis, one that threatened the very future of our planet:

For decades, scientists had been warning about the catastrophic effects of greenhouse gas emissions and the devastating impact they would have on the environment. But for many people, the warnings fell on deaf ears.

It wasn't until the fear of what was to come began to set in that people started taking action. Fear was a powerful motivator, and in the case of the climate crisis, it was the fear of what would happen if we didn't act that finally spurred significant change.

Prominent figures like Al Gore, Greta Thunberg, and David Attenborough helped raise public awareness about the urgency of the climate crisis. They used their platforms to advocate for action and to hold governments and businesses accountable for their impact on the environment.

People began to realize that the climate crisis was not just a problem for future generations to deal with - it was a problem that was affecting us right now, and it was only going to get worse.

The fear of rising sea levels, catastrophic weather events, and food and water shortages drove people to demand action from their governments and businesses. And in response, innovative solutions and technologies began to emerge.

Renewable energy sources like wind and solar power became more efficient and affordable, while electric cars and public transportation systems gained popularity.

People started taking small actions in their daily lives too, like reducing their use of single-use plastics and composting their waste.

The fear of what could happen if we didn't act was the catalyst for this change, and it was a powerful force. But it was also important to acknowledge that fear alone wasn't enough. It was up to all of us to take action, to be proactive and to demand change from those in power.

The climate crisis was not an issue that would be solved overnight. It required a long-term commitment and a sustained effort from everyone. But by harnessing the power of fear and using it to drive action, we could make a real difference and create a more sustainable future for ourselves and generations to come.

CHAPTER 98

THE COLD WAR

During the Cold War, the United States and the Soviet Union were in a constant state of fear-driven competition. This competition extended beyond military might and into the realm of space exploration, with each nation vying to prove its technological superiority. The United States led the Western alliance, which included countries such as the United Kingdom and France, while the Soviet Union led the Eastern alliance, which included countries such as China and Cuba.

In 1957, the Soviet Union launched Sputnik, the world's first artificial satellite, sparking fear and anxiety among Americans that the Soviet Union had surpassed the United States in space technology. This fear led to a massive investment in space exploration by the United States, culminating in the Apollo program which put the first humans on the moon in 1969.

The Space Race fueled remarkable advancements in space technology and exploration, including the development of new rocket propulsion systems, satellites, and space telescopes. It also resulted in significant scientific discoveries and a better understanding of the universe.

However, the Space Race was also driven by Cold War fears, with each nation seeking to prove its technological superiority as a means of gaining geopolitical advantage. The competition was not without its tragedies, including the loss of American astronauts in the Apollo 1 fire and the Soviet cosmonauts in the Soyuz 1 crash.

Overall, the Space Race was a testament to the power of fear as a motivator for technological advancement, but also a cautionary tale of the dangers of fear-driven competition.

CHAPTER 99

DIGITAL AGE THE CYBER THREATS

In the modern digital age, the fear of cyber threats has become a pervasive concern for individuals, organizations, and governments alike. The rise of cyberattacks, data breaches, and other digital security risks has led to a growing sense of vulnerability and fear of the potential consequences of such attacks.

This fear has also sparked significant advancements in cybersecurity technology and strategies, as well as international efforts to protect critical infrastructure and combat cyber threats. Countries such as the United States, Russia, and China have invested heavily in cybersecurity research and development, as well as creating dedicated cyber defence agencies and task forces.

The fear of cyber threats has also led to the development of new policies and regulations aimed at improving digital security. Governments around the world have implemented cybersecurity standards, such as the European Union's General Data Protection Regulation (GDPR), to protect personal data and to prevent cyber attacks.

However, despite these efforts, cyber threats continue to evolve and become more sophisticated, leaving individuals and organizations feeling vulnerable and fearful. High-profile cyber attacks, such as the 2017 WannaCry ransomware attack that affected over 200,000 computers in 150 countries, serve as stark reminders of the potential consequences of digital vulnerability.

Overall, the fear of cyber threats has led to significant advancements in cybersecurity technology and international collaboration to combat these threats. However, the constant evolution of cyber threats highlights the ongoing need for continued innovation and vigilance in the digital security realm.

CHAPTER 100

THE DRIVE FOR MEDICAL ADVANCEMENT

In The Fear of Epidemics and the Drive for Medical Advancements, we explore how pandemics throughout history have caused fear and inspired medical research to develop new vaccines and treatments.

For example, the Spanish flu pandemic of 1918-1919 caused millions of deaths worldwide and led to fear and panic among the general population. In response, scientists worked tirelessly to develop new vaccines and treatments to help prevent and treat the flu.

Similarly, the COVID-19 pandemic that began in 2019 has caused widespread fear and anxiety, leading to an unprecedented global effort to develop effective vaccines and treatments. In record time, multiple vaccines have been developed and approved for use, which is a testament to the power of human innovation and the fear-driven desire to protect ourselves and our loved ones from harm.

The fear of epidemics has driven significant advancements in medical research, leading to breakthroughs in vaccines and treatments that have saved countless lives throughout history.

CHAPTER 101

THE CIVIL RIGHTS MOVEMENT

The Civil Rights Movement was a major social movement in the United States in the 1950s and 1960s, aimed at ending segregation and discrimination against African Americans. One of the driving forces behind this movement was the fear experienced by African Americans due to the pervasive discrimination and violence they faced on a daily basis. Fear of being attacked or killed, fear of being excluded from opportunities, and fear of being treated unfairly were all common among African Americans during this time.

This fear was a powerful motivator for activists who sought to bring about change. For example, Rosa Parks, a civil rights activist, refused to give up her seat on a Montgomery, Alabama bus in 1955 because she was tired of the constant fear and indignity of being forced to sit in the back of the bus due to her race. Her actions sparked the Montgomery Bus Boycott, a year-long protest that ultimately led to the desegregation of Montgomery's public transportation system.

Similarly, the fear of continued discrimination and violence drove many other civil rights activists to take action. The Freedom Riders, for instance, was a group of activists who rode buses across the southern United

States in 1961 to challenge segregation in interstate travel. Despite facing violent opposition, including being attacked by white supremacist mobs, they persisted in their efforts and ultimately helped bring change.

Fear played a critical role in the Civil Rights Movement, motivating individuals to stand up for their rights and fight for justice in the face of overwhelming odds.

In the current context, the Black Lives Matter movement is a prime example of how fear can motivate people to fight for their rights and demand change. The movement was sparked by a series of high-profile incidents of police brutality against Black individuals, which created widespread fear of ongoing systemic racism and violence. This fear led to a groundswell of protests and activism, with people demanding reform of the criminal justice system and an end to racial discrimination.

Another example is the fear of voter suppression and discrimination in the United States, which has driven a surge in voter turnout and activism. In the 2020 presidential election, fears of voter suppression and disenfranchisement among communities of colour and marginalized groups led to record-breaking voter turnout and a widespread movement to protect voting rights and access. This fear of discrimination and disenfranchisement has also sparked ongoing efforts to address gerrymandering, voter ID laws, and other barriers to voting in order to ensure fair and equal access to the ballot box.

CHAPTER 102

THE ECONOMIC POLICY

Fear has played a significant role in shaping economic policy throughout history. For example, during the Great Depression, fear of economic collapse led to President Franklin D. Roosevelt's New Deal, which aimed to stimulate the economy and provide relief to millions of Americans. Similarly, during the Global Financial Crisis of 2008, fear of a widespread financial meltdown led to government intervention, including the Troubled Asset Relief Program (TARP) and other measures designed to stabilize financial institutions and prevent further economic decline.

In the current context, fear of a global economic recession due to the COVID-19 pandemic has prompted government responses around the world. For instance, many governments have implemented stimulus packages to provide relief to struggling individuals and businesses, while central banks have implemented low-interest-rate policies to encourage lending and support economic growth. Additionally, the fear of supply chain disruptions and global economic instability has led to an increased focus on reshoring and domestic manufacturing in many countries.

Overall, fear has been a driving force in shaping economic policy and responding to financial crises throughout history, and continues to play a significant role in shaping economic decisions today.

CHAPTER 103

AN ARTIFICIAL INTELLIGENCE

The fear of artificial intelligence (AI) has been growing in recent years, as people become increasingly concerned about the potential consequences of its widespread use. Many fear that AI could lead to job loss, exacerbate social inequality, and even pose a threat to humanity itself. However, this fear has also sparked an increased focus on the ethics of technology and responsible development.

One example of the fear of AI is the debate surrounding autonomous weapons, or "killer robots." These weapons are designed to select and attack targets without human intervention, and many fear that they could lead to unintended harm or even trigger a global arms race. As a result, there have been international efforts to ban or regulate the development and use of such weapons.

Another example is the fear of AI bias, which occurs when algorithms are trained on biased data sets, leading to discriminatory outcomes. For instance, facial recognition technology has been criticized for being less accurate for people with darker skin tones, which could lead to false identifications and unjust treatment.

To address these concerns, there has been an increased focus on the ethics of technology and responsible development. Some companies and organizations have established AI ethics boards to guide their decision-making, and there has been a push for greater transparency and accountability in the development and deployment of AI systems.

Overall, the fear of AI has led to a greater awareness of the potential risks and ethical considerations surrounding technology and has spurred efforts to develop responsible and beneficial AI systems.

CHAPTER 104

GLOBALIZATION

Globalization is a process of increasing the interconnectedness and integration of economies, societies, and cultures across the world. However, some people fear that globalization threatens their economic, social, and cultural identity and leads to job losses and cultural homogenization.

This fear has contributed to the rise of nationalist movements and protectionist policies in various countries. For instance, the United Kingdom's decision to leave the European Union, commonly known as Brexit, was fueled by fears of uncontrolled immigration, loss of sovereignty, and economic decline. Similarly, the United States under President Donald Trump imposed tariffs on imports from China and other countries, arguing that they were taking advantage of America's open market and stealing jobs from American workers.

Other countries that have seen a rise in nationalism and protectionism include India, where the government has adopted a "Make in India" campaign to promote domestic manufacturing and reduce imports, and Brazil, where President Jair Bolsonaro has pursued a policy of economic nationalism to protect Brazilian businesses and workers.

However, critics argue that nationalism and protectionism can lead to trade wars, reduce global economic growth, and exacerbate political tensions between countries. They also argue that globalization has brought many benefits, such as higher living standards, lower prices, and cultural diversity.

In conclusion, the fear of globalization has contributed to the rise of nationalist movements and protectionist policies in various countries, leading to tensions between nations and potential economic consequences. It is important for policymakers to address the legitimate concerns of their citizens while recognizing the benefits of globalization and promoting cooperation and collaboration between nations.

CHAPTER 105

FEAR OF NUCLEAR CONFLICT

The fear of nuclear conflict has been a significant global concern since the development of nuclear weapons during World War II. The Cold War between the United States and the Soviet Union was characterized by a constant state of fear and tension, with both sides possessing large nuclear arsenals capable of causing mass destruction. The Cuban Missile Crisis in 1962 brought the world to the brink of nuclear war, as the United States and Soviet Union engaged in a tense standoff over the placement of Soviet missiles in Cuba.

Since then, the fear of nuclear conflict has led to various disarmament initiatives and treaties aimed at reducing the risk of global catastrophe. The Treaty on the Non-Proliferation of Nuclear Weapons (NPT) was signed in 1968 and is still in force today, with the aim of preventing the spread of nuclear weapons and promoting disarmament. In addition, the Comprehensive Nuclear-Test-Ban Treaty (CTBT) was adopted by the United Nations General Assembly in 1996, with the aim of banning all nuclear explosions worldwide.

More recently, the fear of nuclear conflict has been heightened by tensions between the United States and North Korea, with the North Korean regime continuing to develop its nuclear weapons program despite international sanctions and pressure. The United States and Russia have also been engaged in a new nuclear arms race, with both countries modernizing their nuclear arsenals and developing new weapons systems.

In response to these fears, there have been renewed calls for disarmament and the elimination of nuclear weapons altogether. The International Campaign to Abolish Nuclear Weapons (ICAN) was awarded the Nobel Peace Prize in 2017 for its efforts to achieve a treaty banning nuclear weapons. While progress has been slow, the fear of nuclear conflict remains a powerful motivator for global action towards disarmament and non-proliferation.

CHAPTER 106

THE FEAR OF OVERPOPULATION

Has been present for decades, with concerns over limited resources and the ability of the planet to sustain a growing population. This fear has led to significant advancements in sustainable development and environmental conservation efforts.

For example, in the 1960s, concerns about overpopulation and its impact on the environment led to the formation of the United Nations Population Fund, which works to improve reproductive health and family planning services. Additionally, the fear of overpopulation has led to innovative solutions such as vertical farming, which allows for more efficient use of limited land resources to produce food.

In recent years, the fear of overpopulation has contributed to the growing awareness of the need for sustainable development and environmental conservation efforts. Initiatives such as the United Nations Sustainable Development Goals and the Paris Agreement on Climate Change reflect the global community's recognition of the need to balance economic growth with environmental sustainability.

Ultimately, the fear of overpopulation has sparked significant action and innovation towards sustainable development, highlighting the importance of balancing economic growth with environmental conservation for the benefit of future generations.

CHAPTER 107

GENETIC ENGINEERING

Genetic engineering and gene editing technologies have revolutionized the field of medicine and agriculture, but they also evoke fear and ethical concerns. The fear of genetically modified organisms (GMOs) and the potential risks associated with them has led to public outcry and protests. The ethical concerns surrounding the use of these technologies in humans, such as designer babies and genetic enhancements, have also sparked debates.

As a response to these fears, bioethics has emerged as a field focused on studying the ethical implications of biomedical and biological research. The field aims to ensure that these technologies are developed and used in a responsible and ethical manner. Bioethics has led to the development of guidelines and policies for the use of genetic engineering and gene editing, such as the International Summit on Human Gene Editing, which called for a moratorium on heritable genome editing.

While genetic engineering and gene editing have the potential to cure diseases and improve agriculture, it is important to consider the potential risks and ethical concerns associated with these technologies. The fear surrounding genetic engineering has led to increased public awareness and debates, ultimately contributing to the development of responsible guidelines and policies.

CHAPTER 108

THE DATA PRIVACY

The fear of personal information being exposed on social media platforms has been a growing concern in recent years, as incidents of data breaches and privacy violations have made headlines. This fear has driven efforts to improve privacy settings on social media platforms and advocate for user control over their data.

For example, in 2018, the Facebook-Cambridge Analytica scandal involved the unauthorized harvesting of millions of Facebook users' personal data to influence political campaigns. This sparked a public outcry and led to increased pressure on social media platforms to improve their privacy practices.

As a result, many platforms have introduced new features to give users more control over their data, such as the ability to limit who can see their posts and activity, as well as tools to manage ad preferences and data sharing. In addition, new regulations such as the European Union's General Data Protection Regulation (GDPR) have been implemented to protect user privacy.

Overall, the fear of personal information being exposed on social media has led to a greater focus on privacy and the need for greater transparency and control over personal data.

CHAPTER 109

THE FEAR OF SCARE RESOURCES

The fear of running out of finite resources such as fossil fuels has driven the search for alternative, renewable sources of energy. Climate change and its potentially catastrophic consequences have further intensified this fear, leading to a global push for clean energy solutions. This has resulted in significant innovation and investment in technologies such as solar and wind power, as well as biofuels and hydrogen fuel cells.

For example, countries such as Germany and Denmark have made significant strides in transitioning to renewable energy sources, with renewable energy accounting for over 40% of their energy consumption. The United States has also seen significant growth in renewable energy, with the solar industry alone employing over 240,000 people. International agreements such as the Paris Agreement, which aims to limit global temperature rise to below 2°C above pre-industrial levels, further emphasize the urgency of transitioning to renewable energy.

Overall, the fear of resource scarcity and the need for sustainable development have driven the pursuit of renewable energy, leading to significant advancements in clean energy technologies and efforts to combat climate change.

Here are some examples of countries and their efforts towards renewable energy in response to the fear of resource scarcity:

China: As the world's largest greenhouse gas emitter, China has made significant strides in developing renewable energy sources. The country is the world's largest producer of solar panels and wind turbines and has set a goal of reaching carbon neutrality by 2060.

Germany: Germany has been a leader in renewable energy for years, with a goal of generating 65% of its electricity from renewable sources by 2030. The country has invested heavily in wind and solar power and has implemented policies such as feed-in tariffs to incentivize the development of renewable energy.

Denmark: Denmark is another country that has made significant progress in renewable energy, with wind power providing over 40% of the country's electricity in 2019. The country has set a goal of reaching 100% renewable energy by 2050.

United States: The United States has also made efforts towards renewable energy, with wind and solar power accounting for over 11% of the country's electricity generation in 2020. Many states have implemented renewable energy goals and policies, and

President Biden has set a goal of reaching net-zero carbon emissions by 2050.

India: India has set a goal of achieving 175 GW of renewable energy capacity by 2022, with a focus on solar and wind power. The country has implemented policies such as feed-in tariffs and net metering to promote the development of renewable energy.

These examples illustrate how the fear of resource scarcity has driven countries to invest in and prioritize renewable energy sources.

CHAPTER 110

FEAR OF POLARIZATION

In recent years, the fear of polarization and divisiveness has become increasingly prominent in many parts of the world. In the United States, for example, political polarization has reached historic levels, with deep ideological divides and a lack of trust in institutions and political leaders. This fear has driven many individuals and organizations to take action towards promoting unity and understanding among diverse groups.

One such example is the "Better Angels" movement, which brings together individuals from across the political spectrum to engage in dialogue and bridge the partisan divide. The group's workshops and events aim to foster empathy, build relationships, and find common ground among people with different political beliefs.

Similarly, in countries such as India and South Africa, movements focused on interfaith dialogue and cooperation have emerged as a response to increasing religious and cultural polarization. These initiatives bring together individuals from different faiths and backgrounds to build relationships and promote understanding.

In China, the government has launched various initiatives aimed at promoting national unity and social harmony, such as the "Chinese Dream" campaign, which emphasizes the importance of shared values and aspirations for the nation's future.

The fear of polarization and division has also inspired many global initiatives aimed at promoting unity and cooperation among countries. For example, the United Nations Sustainable Development Goals (SDGs) emphasize the importance of global cooperation in tackling issues such as poverty, climate change, and inequality.

Overall, the fear of polarization and division has led to a growing recognition of the need for empathy, dialogue, and understanding in promoting social harmony and unity.

CHAPTER 111

THE CULTURAL IDENTITY

The fear of losing cultural identity is a common concern among various communities around the world. The rise of globalization and the spread of Western culture has led to the fear of cultural homogenization and the loss of traditional values, beliefs, and practices.

For instance, in China, the government has been promoting the preservation of traditional culture and heritage through various initiatives, such as the protection of cultural relics and the restoration of historical sites. One example is the restoration of the Great Wall of China, which has been recognized as a symbol of Chinese culture and heritage.

Similarly, in India, there has been a growing concern about the loss of traditional crafts and art forms due to the rise of industrialization and globalization. The government has taken several initiatives to promote and preserve traditional crafts, such as the establishment of handloom parks and handicraft villages, and providing financial assistance to artisans and craftsmen.

In other parts of the world, indigenous communities are also fighting to preserve their cultural heritage in the face of globalization and modernization. For instance, the Maori people of New Zealand have been actively working to preserve their language, traditions, and cultural practices through various initiatives, such as the establishment of Maori language schools and cultural centres.

Overall, the fear of losing cultural identity has led to a renewed focus on preserving and celebrating cultural heritage and traditions, ensuring that future generations can continue to appreciate and learn from the diversity of human culture.

CHAPTER 112

LINGUISTIC DIVERSITY AND CULTURAL HERITAGE

The fear of losing linguistic diversity and cultural heritage has sparked a growing movement to document and preserve endangered languages. According to UNESCO, around 43% of the world's 6,000 languages are endangered, with many at risk of disappearing within the next few generations.

This fear has led to various initiatives aimed at preserving these endangered languages. For example, the Endangered Languages Project is a collaboration between Google and numerous linguistic experts to document and promote endangered languages. The project provides online resources and tools for users to access and learn about these languages.

Similarly, the Living Tongues Institute for Endangered Languages is an organization dedicated to the documentation and revitalization of endangered languages. They work with local communities to create educational materials, training programs, and language revitalization initiatives.

Another example is the Indigenous Language Institute, which focuses specifically on revitalizing Native American languages in the United States. They work with tribal communities to develop language programs, create educational materials, and provide support for language revitalization efforts.

The fear of language extinction has also led to policy changes in various countries. For example, the United Nations General Assembly designated 2019 as the International Year of Indigenous Languages, aiming to raise awareness about the importance of indigenous languages and promote efforts to preserve them. In Canada, the Indigenous Languages Act was passed in 2019 to support the revitalization and preservation of Indigenous languages.

Overall, the fear of losing linguistic diversity and cultural heritage has driven significant efforts to document, preserve, and revitalize endangered languages.

CHAPTER 113

MASS SURVEILLANCE

The increasing use of technology in our daily lives has brought about the fear of mass surveillance by governments and corporations. The possibility of constant monitoring and tracking of our online and offline activities has raised concerns about personal privacy and autonomy. In response to these fears, individuals, organizations, and governments have been pushing for stronger privacy protections and advocating for the use of privacy-enhancing technologies.

For example, in 2013, Edward Snowden leaked classified documents from the National Security Agency (NSA) revealing the extent of the U.S. government's surveillance programs. This sparked a global debate about the balance between security and privacy and the need for transparency and accountability in government surveillance practices.

In the wake of these revelations, privacy-enhancing technologies such as end-to-end encryption, virtual private networks (VPNs), and the Tor network have gained popularity. These technologies allow individuals to communicate and browse the internet securely and anonymously, protecting their privacy from surveillance.

Furthermore, privacy advocates have been pushing for stronger privacy regulations and laws to protect individuals' digital privacy. The General Data Protection Regulation (GDPR) in the European Union, for example, is a comprehensive data privacy law that gives individuals control over their personal data and requires companies to be transparent about their data practices.

In conclusion, the fear of mass surveillance has driven the development of privacy-enhancing technologies and advocacy for stronger privacy protections. It has also sparked a global conversation about the balance between security and privacy in the digital age.

CHAPTER 114

THE EXTINCTION OF THE WILDLIFE

The fear of extinction has driven efforts to protect and conserve wildlife all around the world. With the loss of habitat and increasing human encroachment on natural ecosystems, many species are threatened with extinction. This fear has led to the creation of various conservation programs and initiatives aimed at protecting endangered species and their habitats. For example, in China, the government has implemented a program to protect the giant panda, which was once on the brink of extinction due to habitat destruction and poaching. The program involves the creation of protected areas, the development of artificial breeding programs, and research into habitat restoration. As a result, the giant panda population has increased significantly in recent years.

Similarly, in Africa, there are various conservation programs aimed at protecting endangered species such as rhinos, elephants, and lions. These programs involve anti-poaching efforts, habitat restoration, and community engagement to promote sustainable and responsible wildlife management. The Maasai Mara National Reserve in Kenya is an example of a protected area that has successfully preserved wildlife populations while also providing economic benefits to the surrounding communities through ecotourism.

In addition to these efforts, there are also various wildlife rehabilitation programs aimed at rehabilitating and releasing injured or orphaned animals back into the wild. These programs often rely on the support of volunteers and donations from the public to continue their work.

Overall, the fear of extinction has inspired many people and organizations to take action to protect and conserve wildlife, leading to innovative solutions and a greater awareness of the importance of preserving biodiversity.

CHAPTER 115

THE EXPLORATION OF THE OUTER SPACE

Throughout human history, the fear of the unknown has motivated us to seek knowledge and understanding about the world around us. The exploration of outer space is one such example, as our curiosity about what lies beyond Earth has driven us to develop the technology and expertise necessary to venture into the cosmos.

One of the earliest examples of space exploration can be traced back to the Soviet Union's launch of Sputnik 1, the world's first artificial satellite, in 1957. This event sparked a fear of falling behind in the technological race between the Soviet Union and the United States, known as the Space Race. The competition that ensued led to remarkable advancements in space exploration and technology, such as the first manned mission to the Moon in 1969 by the United States.

More recently, the fear of the unknown has driven humanity to explore Mars, the next frontier in space exploration. In 2020, the United States successfully launched the Perseverance rover, which landed on the Martian surface and began its mission to search for signs of past microbial life and collect samples for future return to Earth.

The exploration of outer space has also driven us to seek answers to fundamental questions about the universe and our place in it. The Hubble Space Telescope, launched by NASA in 1990, has provided stunning images of distant galaxies and deepened our understanding of the universe's origins and evolution.

Despite the significant advancements made in space exploration, the fear of the unknown remains a driving force. The search for Extraterrestrial life, the discovery of new planets, and the development of new technologies to support deep-space missions continue to capture the imagination of scientists, engineers, and space enthusiasts alike.

In conclusion, the fear of the unknown has played a critical role in driving humanity's exploration of outer space. It has led to remarkable advancements in space technology and provided answers to fundamental questions about the universe. As we continue to push the boundaries of what we know, the fear of the unknown will likely remain a powerful motivator for future space exploration endeavours.

TRIUMPH OVER FEAR

The story comes full circle, drawing a conclusion that emphasises the transformative power of the "Fear on Fire" movement and the hope it brings for a brighter future.

A World Transformed: The impact of the "Fear on Fire" movement ripples across the globe, inspiring individuals from all walks of life to confront their fears, embrace vulnerability, and enact positive change in their lives and communities.

Fear as a Catalyst: The narrative shifts to view fear not as an insurmountable obstacle, but as a catalyst for growth, self-discovery, and empowerment, encouraging individuals to face challenges with resilience and determination.

The Power of Unity: The story highlights the importance of collective action and community support, demonstrating how individuals coming together can create a more compassionate, inclusive, and supportive society.

A Lasting Legacy: The "Fear on Fire" movement leaves a lasting legacy, inspiring future generations to confront their fears, embrace vulnerability, and work together to build a better world.

The New Dawn: As the sun rises on a new day, the world is forever changed by the "Fear on Fire" movement, a testament to the indomitable human spirit and its capacity for growth, transformation, and triumph over fear.

In this final chapter, the story of "Fear on Fire" concludes with a message of hope and inspiration.

Fear is a natural emotion experienced by humans and animals in response to a perceived threat or danger. It serves as a protective mechanism to help us stay safe by triggering physical and mental reactions, such as increased heart rate, rapid breathing, and sharpened focus. These responses prepare us to either face the threat (fight) or avoid it (flight).

To manage fear effectively, try these simple tips:

Acknowledge your fear: Accept that fear is a natural part of life and give yourself permission to feel it.

Identify the source: Determine what is causing your fear and assess whether the threat is real or imagined.

Practise deep breathing: When you feel fear, take slow, deep breaths to calm your mind and body.

Shift your focus: Redirect your attention from the fear to the base of breath coming in and going out naturally, in a few seconds the climax of fear will calm down, and even in the immediate real threat it will find a solution.

Seek support: Talk to someone you trust about your fear, as sharing your feelings can help relieve the burden.

Face your fear: Gradually confront your fear in small, manageable steps to build confidence and resilience.

As we close this journey through "Fear on Fire," we hope that you, as a reader, have gained a deeper understanding of the power and potential that lies within fear. While fear can often be a paralyzing force, the stories and examples shared in this book demonstrate that when harnessed and confronted, fear can also be a catalyst for positive change, innovation, and growth.

The diverse range of topics explored throughout these pages illustrates that fear is universal, transcending cultures, industries, and borders. It is our hope that you are inspired to reflect on your own fears and, perhaps, find the courage to face them head-on, using them as fuel to ignite your own transformative journey.

As you move forward, remember that fear is an inherent part of the human experience, but it does not have to define or limit us. By embracing the "Fear on Fire" philosophy, we can collectively strive for a more resilient, innovative, and compassionate world.

Thank you for joining us on this exploration of fear, and we wish you the courage and conviction to turn your own fears into powerful forces for change.

By

Deepak Shahi

'The Ocean in the Drop"

108 Poems

"The Mystery of the Himalayan Yeti"

Guardian of the Power Stone

"Magical Tales of Kids"

100 Stories

"Lyric & Liberation"

100 Rap Songs

(COMING SOON)

ABOUT AUTHOR

Deepak Shahi was born in Nepal to a father serving in the British Army based in Hong Kong. In 1969, his family migrated to Bombay, India, where he later graduated from Bombay University.

In 1997, he moved to the UK and settled in North London. Throughout his career, he travelled to 36 countries, gaining valuable experience and knowledge of different cultures, religions, languages, politics, history, and ways of life. His experiences inspired him to express his thoughts and ideas through writing books.

FINAL THOUGHTS

As we reach the conclusion of "Fear on Fire," it is important to reflect on the essence of living in the shadow of fear. We are all aware of the impermanence of our existence on this planet, and yet, fear has a way of gripping us tightly and preventing us from fully embracing life. But why should we allow fear to dictate our actions and limit our potential?

In this book, we have explored the power of fear and its impact on our lives. We have seen how fear can either paralyze us or ignite a fire within us. It is up to us to make the choice. As we contemplate the brevity of our time here, let us seize the present moment and make the most of it.

Why not live each day as if it were our last? Why not face our fears head-on and use them as stepping stones towards growth and fulfilment? By letting go of fear's grip, we open ourselves up to new experiences, meaningful connections, and endless possibilities.

So, as we turn the final page, let us remember that fear does not have to be our constant companion. Instead, let us embrace each day with courage, passion, and an unwavering determination to make our lives extraordinary. Together, let us choose to live fearlessly and make every breath count.

Thank you for embarking on this journey with me. May the lessons learned from "Fear on Fire" continue to guide and inspire you long after you close this book.

With gratitude,

Deepak Shahi

email: dkslondon@gmail.com

London ,United Kingdom